THE INCOMPARABLE POWER OF A

Christian

The Holy Spirit's Power to Heal, Protect and Perform Miracles, Signs and Wonders

This book is a compilation on a series from my blog
www.Danielelijahjoseph.com

Daniel Elijah Joseph

DEDICATION

To My Lord and Saviour Jesus Christ and my Precious Holy Spirit. The Holy Spirit is my best friend, the greatest teacher/ instructor I have ever had and the lover of my Soul. Thank you Holy Spirit.

'But as for you, the anointing (the sacred appointment, the unction) which you received from Him abides [permanently] in you; [so] then you have no need that anyone should instruct you. But just as His anointing teaches you concerning everything and is true and is no falsehood, so you must abide in (live in, never depart from) Him [being rooted in Him, knit to Him], just as [His anointing] has taught you [to do]' (1 John 2:27 Amplified)

CONTENTS

THE INCOMPARABLE POWER OF A

Christian

The Holy Spirit's Power to Heal, Protect and Perform Miracles, Signs and Wonders

INTRODUCTION

I became a born-again Christian around 21 years ago. I was fortunate to have gotten baptized in the Holy Spirit, with the gift of our prayer language, at an early stage in my Christian walk.

However, it took a while to fully comprehend its importance and to know how to effectively use the gift of praying in the spirit.

God knows the end from the beginning. He knows the challenges we will face as believers. It is important to note that we all have different spiritual battles.

The scripture to illustrate the point that God knows the end from the beginning can be found in the book of Genesis. God created man in His image and likeness; however, in man was male and female. Let's see Genesis 1:27: "So God created man in His own image, in the image *and* likeness of God He created him; male and female He created them" (Amplified).

The Bible also tells us that God said it is not good for man to be alone. This can be found in Genesis 2:18.

It reads, "Now the LORD God said, 'It is not good (beneficial) for the man to be alone; I will make him a helper [one who balances him—a counterpart who is] suitable *and* complementary for him.'"

What I find interesting is that God sees the whole picture. He starts with the end result. In Genesis 1:27, the Bible indicates that man, in whom God created in His likeness and image, constitutes of both male and female.

At the opportune time, God verbally said what part of His original plan was. The Bible goes on to tell us how woman was made from man.

Another fascinating point in God's structure of doing things is that everything was already set in motion. Let me prove this point.

Genesis 2:24 says, "For this reason a man shall leave his father and his mother, and shall be joined to his wife; and they shall become one flesh."

This is the first mention of father and mother in the Bible. At the time, there was only God the Father. What I am trying to say is that God had the blueprint of His creation from the onset. As we have seen, man is made up of male and female. At the right time, he removed female from man and she was called woman.

Fast forward: man will now leave his father and mother and be joined again to the woman who was separated from man in creation, and he will unite and cleave to her (sticking together like glue) and become one again.

To reiterate, God sees and saw everything that was going to ever happen to creation.

God knew the coronavirus (COVID 19) was going to happen, and I didn't know it then, but I now realise that God was always prompting me to be an advocate for the Holy Spirit.

This is so His people will embrace the benefits of the Holy Spirit's power and other gifts, especially for such a time like this (coronavirus).

Unfortunately, I think my message often falls on deaf ears, as I haven't seen changes in churches. They do not preach the importance of the baptism of the Holy Spirit with evidence of speaking in tongues.

God was trying to prepare us for what was to come (COVID 19).

I believe often there is a correlation between our main calling/spiritual gifts and attacks we face. These attacks are mainly spiritual, which is also known as spiritual warfare.

In the last eight years, the spiritual attacks in my life have intensified and praying in tongues has been extremely helpful and beneficial.

Today, we are facing a global pandemic, and my confidence in my protection and safety comes from the promises of God and from praying in tongues. I like to call this combination *The Incomparable Power of a Christian*.

Let me point out that praying in tongues, praying in the spirit, the prayer language and praying in the Holy Ghost all mean the same.

I read many years ago of an evangelist called John G. Lake. God used this individual mightily in the area of healing.

John G. Lake had the revelation and was so confident in the POWER from the Holy Spirit that he allowed bacteria to be put on his hand and (this was observed under a microscope). The moment the bacteria touched his hand, it died instantly.

Praying in the Holy Spirit is a POWER that even most of the Church can't comprehend. A lot of places called churches have missed the cornerstone of our faith, which in my opinion is the Holy Spirit.

Once a person is born again and has received Jesus as Lord and Saviour, the next thing that SHOULD take place is the baptism of the Holy Spirit with evidence of praying in tongues.

In the book of Acts 19:2, Apostle Paul said, "Did you receive the Holy Spirit when you believed [in Jesus as the Christ]?" indicating that it's essential that one must receive the Holy Spirit.

When Jesus was giving the great commission, He said the following:

"These signs will accompany those who have believed: in My name they will cast out demons, they will speak in new tongues; [18] they will pick up serpents, and if they drink anything deadly, it will not hurt them; they will lay hands on the sick, and they will get well." (Mark 16:17)

I want to zero-in on how they will speak in new tongues; again, this means praying in tongues.

Having evidence of praying in tongues doesn't happen at the same time for all people; hence, the emphasis must be placed on the importance of the gift, and the value of the gift in the life of a believer.

As most of us around the world are in a lockdown, and I can certainly feel the fear in the atmosphere, I am making sure I am filled with the Holy Spirit and meditating on God's Word and promises for divine health and protection. When I do this, I feel supernatural and confident that all is going to be well.

It about time we realise that every word of God is important, and we need to imitate the pioneers of the faith, such as Apostle Paul, as He said he wished that we all would speak in tongues (1Corinthians 14:5). He also said that we must earnestly desire spiritual gifts (1 Corinthians 14:1).

From my experience in life and from walking with the Lord, I must confess nothing just happens. From Apostle Paul's verse above, the word *earnestly* is defined "with sincere and intense conviction; seriously."+

Desire is defined as a strong feeling of wanting to have something or wishing for something to happen.

From the definitions of empowering words from the Great Apostle Paul, it is clear that NO promise of God is automatic, so don't be deceived that things just happen; sometimes they do, but God wants us to be full of power and authority and not be "que sera sera" Christians. We are God's workers on Earth.

From my observation and experience in the Christian faith, I have noticed that there two types of Christians. First, there are those who are in a heavy sleep (a coma), according to our Lord Jesus Christ's words in the book of Revelation 3:16, "So because you are lukewarm (spiritually useless), and neither hot nor cold, I will vomit you out of My mouth [rejecting you with disgust]."

The second type of Christians are the awakened ones—those who have had their spiritual awakening experience. My definition of a Christian awakening is having CHRIST FORMED in us. *CHRIST* means the POWER AND WISDOM OF GOD.

Unfortunately, the vast majority of Christians are still in the first category, which is the sleep state, but the good news is, a shift is about to take place. As a matter of fact, the shift has already started.

I like to refer to this shift as "the transfiguration," which means a complete change of spiritual state, i.e., the awakening state.

The Bible talks about the transfiguration of our Lord Jesus Christ in Luke 9. I want to focus and emphasise on the state of Jesus' inner circle of disciples – Peter, James and John. To those not familiar with the story, Jesus took His inner-circle disciples to the mountains, and He (Jesus) went to pray.

As Jesus was praying, the appearance of His countenance became altered (different), and His raiment became dazzling white [flashing with the brilliance of lightning].

The Bible goes on to say that two men were conversing with Him: Moses and Elijah. In verse 31 of Luke 9, it says Moses and Elijah appeared in splendour *and* majesty *and* brightness and were speaking of His exit [from life], which He was about to bring to realization in Jerusalem.

The Bible says that the disciples were heavy with sleep, but when they had fully awoken, they SAW His glory (splendour and majesty and brightness) and the two men who stood with Him.

The point I am trying to make is that until we fully awake as sons and daughters of God, we will not see the glory of God in and around us. We also won't be in the higher state of consciousness to realise the manifestation of God's holy angels all around us.

Jesus put it this way in Luke 9:27: "However I tell you truly, there are some of those standing here who will not taste death before they see the kingdom of God."

We can only see and comprehend the Kingdom of God when we are fully awake and in the higher state of consciousness.

One thing I have realised, if a Christian does not awake (is not hot), there is a tendency that they could perish like a mere man.

To be awoken, Christ MUST be continuously formed in us. Christ is the power and wisdom of God. It's only with the power of the Holy Spirit that we can rebuke, bind and cast away the demonic coronavirus.

What I have noticed in the world is that the glorious power of the Holy Spirit and the Word of God has been hidden from the hearts of the people. When people are comfortable and living in abundance, there is a tendency for people not to have a need for God.

Another factor that would make God and His Word hidden from people is engaging in the occult and dark magic. Automatically, the devil closes people's spiritual eyes, and they become spiritually dead.

My prayer is that as we seek God and plead for mercy, He (God) will soften the hearts of people so they can hear and allow Jesus in.

Hebrew 3:15 says, "Today if you hear my voice do not harden your heart." In the Book of Revelation 3:20, Jesus says, "I stand at the door and knock. If anyone hears my voice and opens the door, I will come in…"

The only way to fellowship with the incomparable power of a Christian (the Holy Spirit) is by first accepting Jesus Christ as Lord and Saviour.

CHAPTER 1

THE POWER OF THE HOLY SPIRIT

As a Christian, we will ultimately spend eternity with our fellow brethren all over the world, as we are all part of the Body of Christ, so when one part of the body is hurting the whole body is affected.

Recently, we have seen an increase of Gun men and terrorist attack Churches around the world.

To be honest, I am sick and tired, of all this evil coming upon my fellow Christians. So I asked the Lord why and how this could be happening. His answer was simple: PRAY.

Christianity in the west is kind of like another Christianity compared to those that practice the faith in the persecuted areas. In as much as I want to be careful in writing this, you and I know what the Bible says: *My house shall be called a house of prayer for all nations.*

Question: Does your church regularly pray for the brethren in other countries, especially in areas where Christians are persecuted around the world?

Does your church have a prayer meeting where you gather together and pray for other brethren around the world?

What we have to remember is that God is not automatic. You and I co-labor with God, and if we want to see results in our world, the answer is simple: PRAY.

I have said this before: NO POWER CAN BE COMPARED TO THE POWER OF THE HOLY SPIRIT. However, there is a price which must be paid for this anointing, and it's called PRAYER.

Education systems around the world, in most countries, have a grading system, so if you are looking for a school, college or university for yourself or your child, you check the ranking system to see how well this educational establishment is doing compared to the rest.

I believe the Body of Christ needs a centralized table, to measure churches. Part of the measurement would be first to compare it to the early Church. Is it a praying church?

No disrespect to any church or leader, but in these end times, we don't need a social church of partying. We need a PRAYING CHURCH.

I don't want to see my brethren suffer when I know by praying, things could and would change. Social problems in our society should be prayed for by the Church.

The world and governments should be seeking the Church for prayers and divine direction. Every evil in any society as we know is from the enemy, and the Body of Christ has authority over the enemy. Body of Christ, please wake up!

The spiritual temperature of any church is measured by the prayer life of the church. We are certainly in unprecedented times – the end times are singing all around us.

Let's do our part so God can do His part.

Our Saviour Jesus Christ did His part, so let's take our prayer life to a 10-times higher level and activate the victory of our resurrected Saviour. Amen.

CHAPTER 2

11 YEARS WITH THE HOLY SPIRIT

Life is really a mystery. Different people have their perception about life, which could either be true or false or in between.

I think its best when our views about life are based on our experience and the revelations given from the Holy Spirit. Often, revelation is given when we are in certain situations. When such insight from above is given to us, what we know can't be shaken.

For the past 11 years, I've been in training with the Holy Spirit. The reason I call it 11 years is because He led me to live in a particular area, which was pretty much in isolation, and He began a work in me. I really found myself during this time. I came to realize I am an introvert, and I learned how I get filled with power from the Holy Spirit, etc.

Towards the end of this period, I began to realize that all we need is the Holy Spirit.

Apostle John got the same revelation and wrote about it in 1 John 2:27 Apostle Paul also said something similar. He didn't receive the gospel from man (Galatian 1:12).

It's only the Holy Spirit who can change and really teach us.

The place I lived was called 7 Hope. I didn't choose it; it's what was available. I intended it to be for a specific purpose, but God had other plans.

Now, 11 is my special number, and God used 11 years to make Himself real to me. I now understand why people in the Bible put their life on the line instead of bowing down (because of the realness of God that they experienced), and I will 100 percent do the same.

It was during this period that I could relate to the emotions of my favorite apostle, Paul, as he wrote his letters. I also came to realize that to get revelation, you must put in certain conditions, which for the most part are not pleasant.

It was also during this period that the Lord opened my eyes. I could easily spot darkness and the false angel of light.

I have seen the mother of spiritual warfare and the Lord delivered from everyone, and He has equipped me as a warrior.

I do forgive those who fired arrows of wickedness at me, but at the same time, I will always fire the arrows back as I believe this is fair and right.

It was during this period that I lost my mum, and I couldn't go to her burial due to reasons best unsaid.

The Christian spiritual walk is real and deep, for there is a lot of deception around in the world, even in the Body of Christ, but only the Holy Spirit can open one's eyes.

The good news is, the closer we walk with God via the Holy Spirit, the more He reveals to us.

There is so much stuff that the Lord will tell one, that you know you are not allowed to tell another, not now anyway. This walk is an interesting journey, to say the least.

I have been pondering on something recently. We get used to spiritual warfare, and a little something in us likes the good fight sometimes, as it motivates us to rip things apart in the spirit and it fuels our prayer life.

I was told boxers get so used to their regular training and fights in the ring that when they retire, it really affects them mentally.

What I am trying to say is that a little part of a spiritual-warfare warrior likes the battle.

To summarise, my 11 years at 7 Hope was where God made me into a warrior. I have experienced that God is greater in me than every evil force in the world.

I like to believe that the enemy used every weapon he had, but the Lord equipped and delivered me from them all.

I know I look very gentle on the outside, but please don't be fooled. There is a lion on the inside, so think twice before you mess with me.

Lord Jesus, thank you for the Cross and for your amazing grace. Now Lord, Please usher in my soul mate.

I always see silly questions on YouTube and listen to interviews, and people are asked if specific actions are sin or not. To clear the air here, whatever the Bible says is final, people's opinions are irrelevant. We go by what the Bible says, period.

Finally, why do some preachers throw up the devil sign? Can we automatically consider you false ministers that Apostle Paul warned us about?

CHAPTER 3

JESUS, THE HOLY SPIRIT CONNECTOR

Jesus said, "I will build MY Church." Therefore, according to the verse in Matthew 16:18, Jesus owns the Church; however, when some people pray, they can't even pray in Jesus' Name.

Jesus said, "Whatever you ask the Father in My Name..." (John 14.13).

One would hear them say, "In the most holy name," or "In his name," etc., but they could be referring to anybody. In fact, if a person can't pray in Jesus' name, especially in a church gathering, please watch carefully, as the person is most probably involved in other powers, besides the Holy Spirit.

Without the Holy Spirit, we have no Church, and without Jesus going to the cross, there would be no Holy Spirit as we know of the Holy Spirit today.

The disciples fled when Jesus was arrested, and after Jesus' death, they went into hiding, but after Acts 1:8, they turned the world upside down with signs and wonders; as a result, we have what we call the Church today.

However, all sorts of things are happening in the Body of Christ today, and the Lord is going to expose everything shortly because many souls are at risk of HELL.

We actually have some churches that get Christians to sell their souls to the devil. For those responsible for this, it would have been better if they had not been born because judgment is coming.

Jesus said, "Love your enemies and pray for them," (Mathew 5.44), so I obey my Lord and Saviour and love my enemies and pray for them.

However, in Matthew 11:12, Jesus heard His Father (God) say the following: [Jesus only said what He heard His Father say] (John 12.49):

"And from the days of John the Baptist until the present time, the kingdom of heaven has endured violent assault, and violent men seize it by force [as a precious prize—a share in the heavenly kingdom is sought with most ardent zeal and intense exertion]."

Another version says, "The Kingdom of God suffers violence, and violence takes by force."

Therefore, I will pray for my enemies and love them, but at the same time…

From experience, if a person doesn't fire the arrows back to the sender, they will keep on attacking. Therefore, if anyone attacks you with witchcraft, find yourself some powerful spiritual warfare prayers and fire back and protect yourself.

We have seen a lot of wonderful Christians die from various accidents such as car accidents, plane crashes, illnesses, etc.

Such horrible incidents were not from God nor His will.

Therefore, I don't care who fires arrows of wickedness at me. Whosoever it is, I will fire back because I MUST fulfil what I agreed with God my Father to accomplish here on earth before I was in my mother's womb.

Also, I am not God, so if you want power/energy, don't come and steal mine. Go to God, and if you can't connect with God because you have sold your soul, then I really don't know what to say, but I will deal accordingly with energy vampires.

CHAPTER 4

CLOTHED WITH POWER
FROM ON HIGH

Tarry, until endued with power from on high (Luke 24: 49b). (Tarry in the Online Cambridge Dictionary is defined as to stay somewhere longer than expected and delay leaving.) The verse just mentioned was to equip the disciples to carry out the Great Commission.

To be endued with POWER is not only necessary for the ministry, but we need it for our personal life.

As a Christian, we are so blessed to have the Holy Spirit, but more importantly, we are blessed to be filled with the Holy Spirit.

I often wonder how some folks live without the Holy Spirit, because as a people, it was not the original intention for us to live without power.

Sometimes, we try to figure out God's perfect will, not only to please our Heavenly Father, but because He knows what's best for us, and He has the right plan for us.

In my journey, there have been people pulling me in different directions. Now, I close most people out and cut them off, but even still, people have ways that they use to manipulate and influence us and enter our heads.

Their methods are pure evil, despicable and of demonic and earthly wisdom. I have spoken about this in the past, and I have zero tolerance for such behavior and people.

One just needs to look up and see such unethical behavior all around, and you will ask yourself how can it be, but it just makes people lose their religion but have a stronger faith in God.

God opened my eyes many years ago, and I didn't like what I saw, and nothing has changed, but one learns their tricks and tactics. You have to have a rebel heart towards their immoral acts and move on.

However, one can rest and be assured of the verse Luke 24:49b: "Tarry, until you receive power from above." With sufficient and required power comes clarity. Power from above also brings light, and this force from the Holy Ghost brings things to our remembrance that God spoke and revealed to us in the past.

Romans 8: 26-28 also confirms this, because by praying in the Holy Ghost, not only do we receive power, but praying the perfect will of God causes all things to work for good because we Love Him (God), and we are also called according to our Father's purpose.

Power from on high (from the Holy Ghost) is all we need for every situation.

Isaiah 10:27b states that it's the anointing that destroys the yoke, but we have been clothed with power from on high; we should not forget the spoken Word. We have to put God's Word to action and on assignment, as His Word will not return void. Amen.

Some of us have come a long way, to be perfectly honest. We just want God's perfect will, and therefore, we need power for clarity. Our prayer should be, if God's not in it, then I don't want it.

CHAPTER 5

THE HOLY SPIRIT APPROPRIATES OUR FREEDOM

Jesus came to set us free: "He whom the Son sets free is free indeed" (John 8:36).

"If you abide in My word [hold fast to My teachings and live in accordance with them], you are truly My disciples, And you will know the Truth, and the Truth will set you free" (John 8: 31-32).

Both of the verses above talk about freedom.

Freedom is defined as the power or right to act, speak, or think as one wants, and the state of not being imprisoned or enslaved.

My question is, how many so-called Christians, including ministers of the Gospel, can genuinely say they are free to speak and preach the accurate word of God?

We need the courage to follow the work of God, and when we have decided to do that, the Holy Spirit empowers us.

We need supernatural power to live the Christian life and to obey the voice of God.

Jesus came to set us free, but many Christians and leaders are in bondage because they have bowed down.

Such preachers and Christians are not at liberty to do or say what the spirit of God is telling them to say (preach) or do.

They have to obey whom they have bowed down to. They have compromised the gospel, and they are puppets. This is sad, but it is the truth.

We see this with so-called Christian artists and also from the pulpit. Ministers must obey their masters from the click. Hence, they can't preach the infallible Word of God. They care less of obeying the voice of God, and I wonder if they can still hear the Lord's voice.

Most of these leaders didn't start out this way, but the enemy came in and showed the dollar bills, and they fell for it.

They didn't have the courage or the faith to resist the devil.

I am not saying it's easy to walk the straight and narrow, but it's what we signed up for when we decided to follow Jesus.

That's why we have to be full of the Holy Spirit. We can do nothing without the precious Holy Spirit.

When Christians bow down, they are used to manipulating others.

Social media is highly used to manipulate people. The face and the voices used are different from the originators of the message, and such people are just being used.

Sometimes I feel sorry for them, because they have compromised their integrity, but they were NOT forced to bow down. It was their choice to sell out and get paid.

History records everything, and so does Heaven, and God will judge whether they remained true and loyal to Jesus Christ, who remained faithful to His Father to the very end.

Our Lord also was tempted by the devil. The difference is, He resisted. Jesus was full of the Holy Spirit, even in His weak state in the wilderness at the time.

People can see, and they can discern the real from the fake.

What I have noticed is that the fake is so crazy persistent. They plan on winning for the devil; that's how they get promoted and given more toys and happy meals.

God is rich in mercy, but we have to repent as there are a lot of souls at risk.

To be honest, I wish I never had to write messages like this, but nevertheless, I have to obey God, my Father, and imitate Jesus Christ, my Lord and Saviour.

CHAPTER 6

THE HOLY SPIRIT GIVES US HOLY CONFIDENCE

The best verse in the Bible to describe the subtitle is the story of King David. Before young David became King of Israel, he was a shepherd boy, looking after sheep.

God always knows the end from the beginning, so it's fair to say even then, God was training David to know Him.

David knew God was always with him through the cultivated relationship and bond he had with God.

One can say David was sensitive towards the Holy Spirit, and from an early age, he knew when the Holy Spirit was on him.

Experiencing the Holy Spirit can make us feel invincible, but care is needed to act humble and sober.

The enemy knows about the power of the Holy Spirit and will do all it can do to cut off the flow.

The enemy will do this by tempting Christians with sin (such as sexual immorality, sex before marriage, etc.)

You and I know we can't survive without the Holy Ghost.

That's why we must stay humble, sober, watchful, and continuously in prayer.

The Bible says, "Touch not my anointed one and do my prophets no harm," but as we know, people have a habit of not obeying God.

One of the reasons God says this is when a person touches a son/daughter of God to harm them, the anointing on them could be so strong and sending an evil arrow back to them could cause maximum damage.

If a person has the nerve to come against a hot Christian (Book of Revelations) spiritually, what can I say but to applaud you for your courage, but its dumb courage.

David had experienced God when he fought with the lion and the bear when looking after his Father's sheep; hence, he became skilled spiritually, but even that was set up.

God will not always take challenges away from us, but He will use them for learning and development because He knows what's ahead.

When Goliath came on the scene, young David at the time was like, "Yo, Goliath, I know you are a giant and stuff, but what comes on me (The Holy Spirit) is 100 times bigger and stronger than you."

King David had the confidence required to get the job done, simply because He had experienced the Holy Spirit in similar situations in the past (with the lion and the bear).

I say all this because the anointing is real and powerful, so to all uncircumcised Philistines, don't hurt yourself. Let me repeat the word again in case you have forgotten: "Touch not my anointing and do my prophets no harm." This can be found in the book of Psalms.

Nobody likes to see folks get hurt, but what do you expect when you act in ignorance and fire wicked arrows? It will always come back to you sooner or later.

It's not the nature of a Christian to hurt anyone. All they do is return wicked arrows back to the sender.

Finally, I can't live without the Holy Spirit, and all attacks are to disconnect one's relationship with the Holy Spirit, but I've news for you: I will fight to maintain my relationship with the Holy Spirit with all I have, even to my last drop of blood. No one can take the place of the Holy Spirit in me, for in Him, I live, move and have my being.

From Prince Harry to Oprah to Katy Perry, people are trying to bring awareness to mental health.

Well, the answer you seek is the Holy Spirit. The Holy Spirit is all you need; we humans have not been designed to live without help from above.

Now, to receive help from the Holy Spirit, we have to have Jesus as our Lord and Saviour, then we get baptized in the Holy Spirit.

We are then given a prayer language, and as we pray in our prayer language, we receive power, and mental illness doesn't have a chance.

So, Prince Harry, to correctly promote mental health awareness, one has to also bring awareness to the perfect answer to the problem at hand, which is the HOLY SPIRIT. Amen.

CHAPTER 7

THE MAGNIFICENCE OF
THE HOLY SPIRIT

Every individual has a different character. In other words, we all have different characteristics.

As humans, I consider it an art to be able to get along with people; however, since we are all distinct from each other, we can't approach nor deal with each person the same.

Everybody has positive and negative characters; therefore, the first wise thing to do when we meet someone is to try and get insight into their behavior, and we all have different ways of doing that.

Even if we don't have our methods of getting a little insight into a person, we have the magnificence of the Holy Spirit.

We can ask the Holy Spirit anything, and He will tell us in His own time, but once He has answered our question, for the most part, we will know that the Holy Ghost has responded to us.

The Holy Spirit knows everything, but we have to ask Him to give the answer we require. Sometimes we may not like the answer and ignore the answer given by the Holy Spirit, but He has still answered.

The good thing about the Holy Ghost is that we can ask for multiple confirmations from Him, and He will continuously give them to us.

Another magnificence about the Holy Spirit is that He takes the struggle out of the Christian walk. All we need to do is be filled with the Holy Spirit.

Instead of pointing out people's shortcomings in living the Christian faith/life, we should put emphasis on people relying on and asking the Holy Ghost for help.

Everything that influences us in our world utilizes a spirit, either good or bad.

The famous Psalm 23 verse 4, "Even though I walk through, the valley of the shadow of death, I will fear no evil, for you are by my side."

I was listening to this in song form, and the verse I just mentioned above jumped out.

Then I started to analyze it. Fear is a spirit; the enemy and evil people can put an evil spirit of fear on another person.

The second part of the verse says, "You are by my side," that is our Lord Jesus Christ through the Holy Spirit.

I have experienced this several times from a particular person (putting a spirit of fear on another; it can often happen in the workplace).

Suddenly, my emotions will change, and I can trace it back to this individual, that whenever I spoke to her, she would put the evil on me, then I obviously started to avoid her.

However, as a Christian, we have the POWER to bind any and every evil spirit in Jesus Name.

In Matthew 16:19, Jesus said, "I give unto thee the keys of the kingdom of Heaven, and whatsoever thou shalt bind on earth shall be bound in Heaven, and whatsoever thou shalt loose on earth shall be loosed in Heaven."

Going back to Psalm 23 verse 4b, the Lord is by our side by the magnitude that we allow Him, which is fellowship.

The remarkable thing about our faith is that we know when the power is on us, and we also know when we need to be recharged.

As a Christian, baptized in the Holy Ghost (I hope), the Holy Spirit is someone we regularly deal with, and He is the Head of our inner circle.

We need to know the character of the Holy Spirit. The Apostle Paul gave us the revelation and called them fruits of the Holy Spirit, and they are as follows:

1. Love

2. Joy

3. Peace

4. Longsuffering

5. Kindness

6. Goodness

7. Faithfulness

8. Gentleness

9. Self-control

Another magnificent thing is that the more we fellowship with the Holy Ghost and are full of the Holy Spirit, all the fruits and characters of the Holy Spirit rub off on us.

The famous saying is true: "We become whom we hang around."

To top all this up, we go back before the fall in the Garden and become the likeness and image of God. All that is required of us is to fellowship with our precious Lord and Savior Jesus called the Christ.

Finally, I leave you with a verse that could shed some light on mental health awareness, which is 2 Timothy1:7, "For God hath not given us the spirit of fear, but of power and of love and of a sound mind."

Therefore, the spirit of fear is from the enemy. That evil kingdom of darkness, namely mental health, has nothing to with God, as the verse above says our association with the Holy Spirit will bring about the Spirit of love, power and a sound mind.

CHAPTER 8

THE GREATEST POWER IN THE WORLD

The title of this chapter is the name of a book by the late Kathryn Kuhlman. The question on most people's mind is, what power?

To answer the question, it's the power of the Holy Spirit. To a non-believer or someone of another faith, it would take more than just making a statement, such as the title of this chapter.

To a Christian, based on what has been read in the Word of God, the Holy Bible, a lot of people would agree that it is the greatest power in the world.

However, the next question would be, is such power still available today?

The answer to the second question is, yes, but what is the state of the Church today?

We probably have more eloquent speakers today than they had in the time of Jesus and the early Church.

However, what we have to realize is that without the signs, wonders, and miracles Jesus performed, no one would have believed in Him or followed Him.

Apostle Paul put it this way in 2 Corinthians 2:4, "My speech and my preaching was not with enticing words of man's wisdom, but in demonstration of the spirit and of power."

If the power still exists, which it does, then there has to be evidence.

In today's twenty-first century Christianity, the criteria for preaching is how good a speaker actually is.

However, in the early Church, people like Stephen were chosen based on their power and faith (Acts 6:8). Stephen, full of faith and power, did great wonders and miracles among the people.

What I have observed in my Christian journey, of over 20 years, is the power doesn't come easy; it's a full-time commitment, and there is a considerable price to be paid for this anointing.

Part of the price to be paid for such power is being a target to the enemy, as a person then becomes a danger to the enemy's kingdom and spiritual attacks will be the norm.

If a person is a Christian and doesn't face any warfare, then such a person is not a threat to the enemy and will fall into the category of a cold or lukewarm Christian (Revelation 3:16).

It's a good thing for a Christian to be at rest and peaceful; however, to get this state of mind, such a person must have labored in prayer.

When we labor in prayer, we are accumulating power. Nothing works in the Christian faith without power. A sermon can only lift a person's spirit for a short period. What sustains us is the power of the Holy Spirit.

When a person has power on them, or knows how to acquire power, there is a calmness about them, and consequently, they have their eyes on the higher realm of the Spirit.

When we have our eyes on things above, we can get a little cheeky and say what Jesus said in John 8:23, "You are from below, I am from above; you are of this world, I am not of this world." We shouldn't say things like that, as we should be perceived as humble.

On the other hand, honestly, when power is on a person, that's how a person feels.

This power is the most enormous power in the world, and people that flow in it can be a real blessing to the Body of Christ. However, there is too much politics in the Body of Christ.

Jesus chose fishermen and tax collectors, and He then said, "Follow me." Elijah likewise said to Elisha, "Follow me." People followed, and the rest was history.

In our world today, it's the opposite. People will manipulate you into following them, do some witchcraft (such as calling a person's spirit in their sleep to come to their Church), do dark magic to steal people's power and blessing. (Don't worry, I am not mentioning names.)

If only we could copy our Lord and Saviour, the early Church, and the Prophets in the Bible, we would change the world.

The easy way out is only beneficial in the short-term, and everything is being recorded in the history books.

If the Church can try and live up to its potential, most hospitals will be nearly empty.

CHAPTER 9

THE HOLY SPIRIT ENFORCES GOD'S GRACE.

In life, many people have done things they didn't initially believe they could do and achieve, or many of us have endured pain, and looking back, we say, how did I go through that? How did I survive that period?

The answer to the above could be termed as God's grace. Then, as I always like starting with questions, the obvious question is, what is grace?

Before I start with the biblical definition of grace, in the Bible, God often asks His messengers what they saw. One of the ways God communicates to us is through what we see. He uses pictures to reveal more profound things to us.

Anyway, back to grace. According to Wikipedia, grace is described as a gift from the Heavenly Father given through His Son, Jesus Christ. The word grace, as used in the scriptures, refers primarily to the enabling power and spiritual healing offered through the mercy and love of Jesus Christ. The grace of God helps us every day.

As an enabling power, we can do the impossible and endure those hard situations in life that no one is immune from, but it's how we handle such situations that determines if we become stronger as a result of it or if it breaks us.

Grace is also referred to as divine influence. The title of this chapter is called "The Holy Spirit enforces God's grace." The reason I say this is that I see grace as a component of the Holy Spirit. If a person is spirit-filled, then grace will be automatic. They will have confidence to do the impossible and strength to endure challenging times.

Grace can also be perceived as the mercy of God. We see in scriptures, in Ephesians 2: 8, "For by grace are ye saved through faith; and that not of yourselves: it is the gift of God: Not of works, lest any man should boast."

The above depicts the mercy of God, and the famous song "Amazing Grace" is about God's mercy.

In as much as it's incredible and great to walk with the Lord, one has to be careful not to let pride kick in.

The reason I say this is that when God's power is on us, a person can feel invincible from not just the power but also from the by-products of the anointing, such as revelation and the knowledge of spiritual things.

The Bible says knowledge puffs up, but love builds up (1 Corinthians 8:1).

Puffed-up means someone is proud of themselves and they think they are very important.

Another version says while knowledge makes us feel important, love strengthens the Church.

So, may we always walk in Love and try and introduce people to the Holy Spirit. I think street preachers should bear this in mind. Most people have missed the mark, but it's only the power of the Holy Spirit that can change a life, as the Holy Spirit did to us.

A powerful part of scripture that explains my point of us not being prideful of our benefits of walking with God Almighty is found in 2 Corinthians 12: 1-10.

It's impossible to write about God's grace without mentioning the experience of the great Apostle Paul, on the road to Damascus, as this was the beginning of his journey with God, and we know God changed his name from Saul to Paul.

Talking of name change, God did the same to me. God gave me the grace to proceed with what he told me instead of focusing on the repercussions in the natural.

Then, when He gave me instructions, I simply obeyed. It was later that I began to understand the reason.

Now my name to me signifies power and a person with a relationship with the creator of the universe.

Some people still call me by my old name, which depicts culture and tradition. That person is a new man in Jesus Christ, but I leave those who call me by my old name to their disrespectful self. Old things have passed away; all things have become new. Amen.

Before I get carried away, let's look at the verse I promised. Many of us are aware the Apostle Paul's incident, and the thorn in his flesh. There are a few interpretations of the spiritual meaning of the verse, "My grace is sufficient." Some say it means God, saying sort it out yourself, which I totally disagree.

The reason is simply in as much as we could have strong faith, we still pray to God in Jesus' name. Period!

To really understand this piece of scripture, we have to take it from the beginning of the chapter, so let's do that.

2 Corinthians 12:1-10 Amplified Bible (AMP)

"It is necessary to boast, though nothing is gained by it; but I will go on to visions and revelations of the Lord. 2 I know a [a]man in Christ who fourteen years ago—whether in the body I do not know, or out of the body I do not know, [only] God knows—such a man was caught up to the [b]third heaven. 3 And I know that such a man—whether in the body or out of the body I do not know, [only] God knows— 4 was caught up into [c]Paradise and heard inexpressible words which man is not permitted to speak [words too scared to tell]. 5 On behalf of such a man [and his experiences], I will boast; but in my own behalf I will not boast, except in regard to my weaknesses. 6 If I wish to boast, I will not be foolish, because I will be speaking the truth. But I abstain [from it], so that no one will credit me with more than [is justified by what] he sees in me or hears from me."

A Thorn in the Flesh

"7 Because of the surpassing greatness and extraordinary nature of the revelations [which I received from God], for this reason, to keep me from thinking of myself as important, a thorn in the flesh was given to me, a messenger of Satan, to torment and harass me—to keep me from exalting myself! 8 Concerning this I pleaded with the Lord three times that it might leave me; 9 but He has said to me, "My grace is sufficient for you [My lovingkindness and My mercy are more than enough—always available—regardless of the situation]; for [My] power is being perfected [and is completed and shows itself most effectively] in [your] weakness." Therefore, I will all the more gladly boast in my weaknesses, so that the Power of Christ [may completely enfold me and] may dwell in me. 10

So I am well pleased with weaknesses, with insults, with distresses, with persecutions, and with difficulties, for the sake of Christ; for when I am weak [in human strength], then I am strong [truly able, truly powerful, truly drawing from God's strength]."

In other words, God knows how to keep us balanced. I mentioned that walking with God and having the anointing and power can make a person feel superior to others. Consequently, pride can kick in.

We also know that God resists the proud but gives grace to the humble.

Apostle Paul's thorn in the flesh was to keep him humble. God has to keep us humble so that He can use us.

It's not about us, but to God be the glory. We are partakers in God's divine nature, but we can do nothing without Him.

Some prayers haven't been answered for the simple reason that God's timetable is perfect; it's not always a faith issue.

I conclude with this: when we are weak in human strength, we are strong in God's strength.

We must keep on being diligent in prayer and trust God's timing. Amen.

CHAPTER 10

THE HOLY SPIRIT IN US AND ON US.

When a person receives Jesus Christ as Lord and Saviour, part of the package is the Holy Spirit. The Holy Spirit comes and lives inside the believer.

In the Old Testament, the Holy Spirit came upon them for specific activities and services ordered by the Lord.

However, there is a principal in both the Old and New Testament, which is, if we draw near to the Lord, He will draw near to us (James 4:8).

I would also like to compare the Holy Spirit on us in the Old Testament as us being filled with the Holy Spirit.

A born-again Christian with the Holy Spirit living on the inside could still end up being a cold and lukewarm Christian.

If a Christian after conversion does not draw near to God, then in as much as the Holy Spirit technically should be living on the inside, such a person may not sense God's presence because they are not drawing near to God.

People like Joshua and Caleb would have had a regular devotion with God; hence, that made them have a different Spirit compared to the other leaders who went to spy the land.

In Numbers 14:24, the Bible says, "My servant, Caleb hath followed me fully." Another version says *wholeheartedly*.

To follow God fully and wholeheartedly requires regular fellowship.

God actually takes account of this as the Bible says in 2 Chronicles 16:9

2 Chronicles 16:9 Amplified Bible (AMP)

"9 For the eyes of the LORD move to and fro throughout the earth so that He may support those whose heart is completely His."

God definitely has to support us because the closer we draw to God, the more we face attacks. The enemy will try every trick in the book to get a Christian to his dark kingdom.

The question is, how do we survive these last days when our every step is watched and our every conversation is being listened to?

To answer the above question, there is another verse in the Old Testament, in 2 Chronicles 15:2, that we can find rest in.

2 Chronicles 15:2 Amplified Bible (AMP)

"Hear me, Asa, and all Judah and Benjamin: the LORD is with you while you are with Him. If you seek Him [inquiring for and of Him, as your soul's first necessity], He will let you find Him; but if you abandon (turn away from) Him, He will abandon (turn away from) you."

We can replace the names above (Asa, Judah, and Benjamin) with our name, seeking God as our soul's first necessity.

When we are seeking God always, God's Spirit will not only be with us but also on us (filled with the Holy Spirit). The hand of the Lord will be on us.

I will write about ways on how to be filled with the Holy Spirit in the next chapter (the Holy Spirit on us, as I like to put it).

The Holy Spirit has to be active in the life of a Christian, not dormant, and I believe that's why Apostle Paul told Timothy in 2 Timothy 1:6 to fan the flame of the gift of God.

It is what it is, and we have to do what we have to do.

It is the Spirit who gives life; the flesh profits nothing (John 6:63). A non-Christian seeing this verse might be asking what in the world does this means.

My understanding of this verse is that the real us is Spirit, and when our Spirit connects to the Holy Spirit (this can only happen when we become born again), then the supernatural comes on us, enabling us to operate in a higher dimension, which our flesh would never be able to achieve or comprehend.

A robust, powerful spirit can carry our physical body and fix all the defects that it has (healing). This can happen by a spoken word and by the laying on of hands and thoughts (as a man thinks, so is he).

The flesh can't do that. A person might be good-looking with all the money in the world, but he / she has limitations.

When our spirit is connected with the Holy Spirit, and filled with the Holy Spirit of Almighty God, anything can happen. It's exciting when such words are preached, and it gets folks clapping and shouting, but often times, no one mentions the price that must be paid to acquire such awesome power (amount in terms of lifestyle to walk with God). It gets lonely sometimes, but the power is real.

The reason it gets lonely is because one tends not to trust anyone. A person would have seen a lot of fake folks and liars along their journey.

Biblically it is not a bad thing not to trust people as in the book of Jeremiah it says the following

Jeremiah 17:5, 7 Amplified Bible (AMP)

5: Thus says the LORD,

"Cursed is the man who trusts in and relies on mankind,

Making [weak, faulty human] flesh his strength,

And whose mind and heart turn away from the LORD."

7: **"Blessed** [with spiritual security] is the man who believes and trusts in and relies on the LORD

And whose hope and confident expectation is the LORD."

The two above verses will be forced on you by life's experience, once you have seen the lies, manipulation and the dark magic humans use. No one will teach you never to trust in man, as you will know that your trust has to be in God only.

This section is about how to be filled with the Holy Spirit.

Now, there is a war going on within every human being. This insight has been given to us by the great Apostle Paul in the book of Galatians.

Galatians 5:17 International Standard Version (ISV)

"17 For what the flesh wants is opposed to the Spirit, and what the Spirit wants is opposed to the flesh. They are opposed to each other, and so you do not do what you want to do."

There will always be opposition, an evil spiritual resistance, that doesn't want a person to embrace fellowship with God.

Such distractions are planned by the enemy of our soul. When we start to fellowship with God, we will ultimately be one with God, as Jesus said He and His Father are one.

When we are one with God, we see differently. The Holy Spirit begins to open our eyes.

The enemy doesn't want this to happen because he wants to control the people with distractions, such as television, social media, computer games, having fun, etc.

All these distractions take people's power and blinds the spiritual eyes of the masses.

The distractions mentioned above have been designed to feed the flesh, which then makes us weak and not strong in spiritual things, and we can then say the flesh is weak, even if the Spirit is willing.

Matthew 26:41.

"Watch and pray, so you don't fall into temptation, for the Spirit is willing, but the flesh is weak."

How to be filled up with the Holy Spirit of God

To be filled with the Holy Spirit starts with what we feed our senses, such as hearing and sight.

Hearing is what we listen to, what type of music and the message of the music one listens to. This affects our Spirit and soul. You can listen to an audio Bible, which is suitable for one's Spirit (powerful).

Sight, is what type of movies we watch. The kind of television a person watches says a lot about the person. The less TV, the better (no TV is best), but that's a personal decision. What we watch also affects our soul and Spirit.

Devotion and Prayer. One should have a regular time of prayer and of reading the Word of God. The most enormous power in the world comes from praying. It's also good to **add fasting**, depending on one's schedule at any point in time.

Finally, ask for the **baptism of the Holy Spirit** with evidence of praying in tongues. This was the **secret to the Great Apostle Paul's power**, and he did it a lot.

I do get a lot of spiritual attacks writing about this topic, so please keep me in prayer.

CHAPTER 11

THE HOLY SPIRIT SPEAKS AND SEERS SEE

It would be a shame to walk through life without having a relationship with the Holy Spirit.

In a world where people are laying snares and traps left, right and center, without having the Holy Spirit in one's corner, the enemy of one's soul will knock a person down for six.

People want to steal and transfer other people's virtues; you can't trust anybody.

The Holy Spirit will reveal all the plans of the enemy; all we need to do is ask.

Seers see supernaturally with the help of the Holy Spirit, and I know not everybody is a seer, but the Holy Spirit will show and tell us all we need to know.

As I have said before, my motto is zero tolerance for witchcraft, and this will not change, and I don't care who the folks are who perform this dark magic.

There are a lot of Esau's in the world who will sell their spiritual gift for material gain, but once a person knows that this world is temporary, then such dumb acts will be far from a person's mind.

Others will aid and abet to steal other people's virtues and gifts, which is why we need the Holy Ghost.

Last week, I got hit by at least 3 different groups from the kingdom of darkness. The Holy Spirit revealed them all, and as a seer, I can also see stuff supernaturally.

The more one gets these attacks, it just gives one the determination to follow Jesus to the end.

The cross before me

The world behind me

If none go with me, still I will follow

No turning back. **No turning back.**

I have decided to wholeheartedly follow my **Saviour Jesus Christ. (No compromise.)**

Again, going back to my previous chapter, walking with the Lord can be lonely, not just because one doesn't trust anyone, but the Holy Spirit reveals who people are and their intentions.

God gives a gift to specific people for a reason, **not to be stolen or transferred by others.** That's why we have to take **complete ownership of the spiritual gifts we have.**

God doesn't make mistakes. He gives specific gifts to certain people for a reason.

God, in His infinite wisdom, set some people apart before they were born **(Jeremiah 1.5)**, so let it be. If you are in spiritual ignorance, turn to Jesus for light.

Sometimes, I ask myself, can this world get any darker? To be honest, I don't know. All I say is, come to Lord Jesus, yes, come quickly.

Just a couple of days ago, I was mad at folks who attacked me, but it's as if God gave me a revelation that we don't fight against flesh and blood.

In other words, the physical people who attack us are sent by their father the devil (the same created being who got kicked out of Heaven).

So, I genuinely forgive these folks. However, I have to protect myself, and consequently, I let the wall go back up towards these people, because one just needs to ask the Holy Spirit who is attacking, and He will reveal.

Again, I am not mad. I will keep on praying for my enemy's soul and for their salvation.

There is going to be a new Heaven and Earth, and if Jesus is not your Lord and Saviour, you will not be part of it.

So, why not shame the devil and his demons that God created Hell for and come to the Light of Jesus Christ?

CHAPTER 12

THE HOLY SPIRIT WILL TEACH US TO FISH

There is a famous saying that goes like this: Give a man a fish, and you feed him for a day. Teach a man to catch fish, and you feed him for a lifetime.

Going through this Christian journey, one experiences a lot of church practices or the norms of Christianity such as breakthrough church service, deliverance from demonic oppression, etc, which are all good.

However, a lot of these practices can be done by oneself. The reason I say this is because as the world is getting darker and darker, attacks can sometimes happen by the second or by the hour, depending on the magnitude of a threat one is to the enemy.

So, what I'm saying is that if a person knows how to discipline oneself, and when they sense that they are under attack, they should know the right prayers to counterattack their attack.

What good is it if one travels a long journey for deliverance or for a breakthrough service but the moment you get home, one is attacked again by the kingdom of darkness?

In my opinion, I think it makes perfect sense that great books are written on these topics so people can deliver themselves from demonic oppression and grow in the Lord. All one needs is the discipline and right tools to pray (specific prayer points).

We should never forget that we have been **given authority over the kingdom of darkness** and we must pray in **faith in Jesus' NAME.**

I believe there are good books out there on prayer warfare.

One cannot afford to depend on someone else for their deliverance. Like the fish saying goes, if you give a man a fish, you feed him for the day or for the moment, but if you teach him to fish or to catch fish, you feed him for a lifetime.

Christians need to be taught how to pray appropriately so they can deliver themselves from demonic oppression.

One thing is for sure, the Holy Spirit will direct us to the right source to get the materials that we need at any point in time. What I've noticed is that different churches and ministries specialize in various aspects of our spiritual needs.

In other words, some churches and ministries have a deeper understanding of certain aspects that we face as Christians.

Therefore, it's vital that we're not close-minded and that we lay hold of the materials the other churches and ministers produce.

We don't need to jump ship and change the churches; all we need to do is get hold of required materials such as prayer books and use them.

By using them, we will grow spiritually, and we can also be a blessing to others because of the spiritual knowledge we have acquired by using these books and prayer materials.

We have the Holy Spirit, and direct access to God, so let's start praying the right and correct prayer points.

CHAPTER 13

THE HOLY SPIRIT MAKES US BOLD

When we cling to the Holy Spirit and look up as a child to Jesus, our Lord, it's fair to say we are with Jesus.

As we see in **Acts 4:13**, Peter and John acted in boldness. The rulers of the people and the elders of Israel perceived that they were uneducated and untrained men and they marveled, and realized they had been with Jesus.

Peter and John were **full of the Holy Spirit** but uneducated and untrained, and they performed signs and wonders and people followed them.

We have the Holy Ghost with us, so we should be able to **demonstrate the POWER of God** as Peter and John, especially those in full-time ministry.

The reason I said especially those in full-time ministry is that to really flow in power, one has to be a person of prayer. Those in **full-time ministry** have more time to focus on the things of God.

As a matter of fact, that's one of the secrets of the early Church: they prayed a lot (they spent hours in prayer). **People in full-time ministry should be able to pray a minimum of 5 hours a day.**

The most apparent difference between the early Church and the twenty-first-century Church is **prayer**; they knew there was **no easy way out**.

God doesn't change. What He did thousands of years ago, He can do today.

When we become a people of **absolute prayer**, we have **faith to receive** and we have an **expectant spirit**.

If we are hungry for an **outpouring of God's power**, it will manifest (our part is to pray).

I believe as a people, we have to be sensitive and focused on the Holy Spirit to be full of the Holy Spirit. It requires 100% focus and commitment.

Everything in life and spiritual issues are according to **(according to the Power according to your faith)** what we put in is what we get out.

I know sometimes we can be given special grace, and God does something special in our midst, but for the most part, what we put in will equal what we get out.

God will raise a group of people in these last days whose number one objective is to seek the Lord Day and Night via prayer and in the Word, and this is how the early Church will be emulated.

I know it's essential for Christians to understand the spiritual climate we are in at the moment, and we are super aware of the darkness and their tricks and traps, but to be honest, we should focus more on our awesome God, our Saviour, and the Holy Spirit.

The Greater one indeed lives in us, and we have to activate this greater power, by being in the Word and in prayer. Remember, it's not automatic.

This life is a preparation for the next. The Book of Revelation, Chapter 21, talks about the **New Heaven and the New Earth** as the first Heaven and Earth will pass away.

CHAPTER 14

THE HOLY SPIRIT SHOWS US GOD'S PATTERN OF DOING THINGS

We don't really hear much of the **New Heaven and New Earth** being preached about. If we ponder on this, then this world will start to make sense.

It's like what God does first is not His perfect plan, but just a build-up, to what He originally had in mind. After all, God knows all things, past present and future.

We see this pattern with the first man, Adam, and the second Adam, Jesus.

Wikipedia states the following:

"The Last Adam, also given as the Final Adam or the Ultimate Adam, is a title given to Jesus in the New Testament. Similar titles that also refer to Jesus include Second Adam and New Adam."

Twice in the New Testament, an explicit comparison is made between Jesus and Adam. In **Romans 5:12–21**, Paul argues that "just as through the disobedience of the one man the many were made sinners, so also through the obedience of the one man the many will be made righteous" **(Romans 5:19, NIV).**

In **1 Corinthians 15:22**, Paul argues that "as in Adam all die, so in Christ, all will be made alive," while in verse 45 he calls Jesus the "last/ ultimate/final Adam."

Therefore, since Jesus was slain before the foundation of the world, one can say God knew Adam was going to mess up, and **God had a contingency plan in place.**

We also see a similar pattern with the **first king of Israel. Saul** was the first king; obviously, he messed up, but God had his eyes on **David.**

David became king and replaced King Saul. Again, as God knows the end from the beginning, it's fair to say God knew Saul would not follow his directions and was preparing King David.

One could also say God saves the best for last.

Again, we see our **current Heaven and Earth** and later the **New Heaven and Earth.**

The first work of God is always a setup for the second, which tends to be perfect.

It seems God starts with a **preliminary.** *Preliminary* is defined as preceding or done in preparation for something fuller or more important.

The Old Testament was a setup for the New Testament; **our current Earth** has been set up for the **New Earth.**

If the New Earth and New Heaven are used as an evangelistic concept, then people could understand that this current world is to prepare us for the next.

The Bible says the following:

Zechariah 13:8 Amplified Bible, Classic Edition (AMPC)

"8 And in all the land, says the Lord, two-thirds shall be cut off and perish, but **one-third shall be left alive**."

Jesus put it this way

Matthew 24:35 Amplified Bible (AMP)

"35 Heaven and Earth [as now known] will pass away, but My words will not pass away."

Therefore if a person is really spiritual and sensible, doesn't it make sense to make sure that **one is part of the one-third** who will make it and **live forever in the new Earth?**

God always starts from the end in mind, and we are filling in the in-between (gaps).

I don't think the filling-in parts is fixed. However, the end result is.

Ephesians 1:4 states: "He has chosen us in Him before the foundation of the world."

The Bible also says in **Revelation 13:8b** that the Lamb (Jesus) was slain before the foundation of the world.

There are things that our created mind can't comprehend; however, if Jesus was slain before the foundation of the world, then God knew the former Archangel Lucifer (God created it), also called the devil, would mess up and be kicked out of Heaven.

The Bible also says that Jesus came to destroy the works of the devil (**1 John 3:8**)**.** Jesus has handed the baton to His followers, and our weapons are the power in the Name of Jesus, the Blood of Jesus and the power and fire of the Holy Spirit.

As nothing could technically overcome Jesus, He has the power over all creation; we have to continue the work, as He has given us the authority and the precious Holy Spirit.

The same pattern can be seen with Jesus choosing His disciples. He knew one was going to betray Him; all of it was part of the Father's plan.

Therefore, one could say God created this world to sift people for the New Heaven and Earth. We also have to realize there is a process in God's way of doing things.

We see this when He planned for the children of Israel to be in Egypt as slaves for **400 years** (God gave Abraham the vision) (**Genesis 15:10).**

God raised Moses to deliver them, and they were in the wilderness, and most of the people died off in the wilderness, as we all have to go through God's sifting process.

The current Earth is similar. God is going sift people out, and they wouldn't make the New Heaven and New Earth.

Science tends to call it climate change or something, but the Bible in **2 Peter 3:10b** says that the elements will melt away.

The elements are melting now, and we call it climate change.

The question is, why don't people believe in God's word?

The Bible says in **2 Corinthians 4:4** that the god of this age (the devil kicked out from Heaven) has blinded the minds of unbelievers so they cannot see the light of the gospel that displays the glory of Christ, who is the image of God.

One thing I have noticed is that some people who don't believe in God practice witchcraft. The moment a person goes into dark magic, their eyes and mind get blinded to the light.

"God is love, and **God** so **loved** the world that He sent His **only Son** and that whomsoever believes in Him shall not perish but have **eternal life" (John 3:16).**

This eternal life is the New Heaven and New Earth.

The choice is yours. Tomorrow might be too late.

Accept Jesus Christ in your heart today, as your Lord and Saviour. Ask Him to forgive you for your sins and repent.

To repent, one needs the Holy Spirit. No one can change from their wicked ways without the help of the Holy Spirit.

Ask God to give you the gift of the Holy Spirit. That's the necessary power to live this Christian life.

CHAPTER 15

THE HOLY SPIRIT AS OUR DECISION MAKER

The greatest fight for every human being, especially a Christian, is the battle for one's SOUL.

Every decision should be based around the premise of, is my soul safe in this direction, place, or with this person?

If you don't feel your soul is safe, then keep your distance.

Sometimes, material things could be used to entice a person's direction, so just be super careful and stay close to the Holy Spirit for clarity.

On Earth, without having the **mark of the beast**, or part of the click, one is **disadvantaged**.

However, **in the afterlife**, those that have the **mark of the beast will be tormented day and night forever (Revelation 14:9-12).**

I look back at every spiritual battle I have engaged in, and the majority of them involve the enemy going after someone's soul.

I'm not going to go into details in regard to those after one's soul, but we all need a reasonable time of reflection with the Holy Spirit, so He can reveal things to us.

God created man in His image. God is pure Light, and to complete the process, God had to have darkness.

"I form the Light and create darkness" (**Isaiah 45:7**).

To create means to bring something into existence—something that had no prior existence.

To form means to mold something already existing into a desired shape.

Genesis 1. 1-3

In the beginning, God created the heaven and the earth.

2 And the earth was without form and void, and darkness was upon the face of the deep. And the Spirit of God moved upon the face of the waters.

3 And God said, Let there be light: and there was light.

From the above verses, God created first; the earth was utterly empty.

God created darkness as part of the process for His final intention.

With no darkness, we can't recognize light. Therefore, the war in Heaven didn't catch God by surprise because it was part of His plan.

To be pure light, God has to create darkness. One can say the darkness is needed to test the light. So we will be tested by darkness and evil (we will be tempted).

We will be tested just like gold is tested by fire.

As I have already indicated, this current earth is for **sifting** out the pure and true light.

God gave us Jesus as the light of the world; believing in Jesus and in His pure light is transferred to those who believe in Him.

Pure light can also be called holy, and the Bible says, "Be holy as I am holy" (**1 Peter 1:16-17).**

Also, the Bible says without holiness, no one can see the Lord (**Hebrews 12:14).**

In as much as we have a role to play, our faith in Jesus, in His blood, and in the Holy Spirit helps us attain the required standard by God.

It's impossible to be what God wants us to be without Jesus dying on the cross and taking our sins away (past, present and future). It's all under the blood. **Praise God!**

Jesus has done most of the work and requirement of God for us to be part of the New Heaven and the New Earth.

The New Heaven and the New Earth are the completeness of God's original intention, and then we will be complete too.

We will be in the complete stage of God creating man in His image in the New Heaven and the New Earth.

At the moment, we are a work in progress; we are in transition.

"He who began a good work in you will continue until the day of Jesus Christ [right up to the time of His return], developing [that good work] and perfecting and bringing it to full completion in you" (**Philippians 1:6).**

In conclusion, Apostle Paul, in **1 Corinthians 13:12b** states:

"For now [in this time of imperfection] we see in a mirror dimly [a blurred reflection, a riddle, an enigma], but then [when the time of perfection comes we will see reality] face to face. Now I know in part [just in fragments], but then I will know fully, just as I have been fully known [by God]."

Perfection is the New Heaven and the New Earth, God's original plan still in process. The devil, darkness, and the Cross are all part of the plan.

The world's population as of today is **7.7 billion.** According to the word of God, only one-third are going to make it to the New Heaven and the New Earth. That is **2.6 billion** as of today's population.

The rest, unfortunately, are going to perish.

Personally, I have been around the block. I have seen, experienced and observed, and I can confidently say **JESUS CHRIST IS THE ONLY ANSWER AND ONLY WAY;** obviously, that's my opinion, and I am entitled to one.

There is a great battle for one's soul. We have to get our priorities right. I know it's not easy, but it will be worth it, and we WILL make it in Jesus' name. Amen.

CHAPTER 16

THE HOLY SPIRIT STILL BRINGS OUT THE FINEST ANOINTING

As Christians, we often hear folks say, "**Lord, do it again.**" Basically, what they mean is that God should perform a **breakthrough/miracle** that they have seen Him do in the past, which is all well and good.

However, what we want to see again is what He (God) did in the early Church, for instance, in **Acts 19.**

The reason I titled of this chapter "The Holy Spirit still brings out the finest anointing" because this impression was laid on my heart when I read **Acts 19.**

The power around today in some gatherings is **polluted.**

This pollution is a result of kundalini spirits, evil spirits, witchcraft, familiar spirits, etc. You name it, it's around in these **last days** of religion in the Church.

It's my **custom** never to **mention names** because if not for **grace,** I would not be standing.

I have experienced all the above evil forces in churches that affect the **flow** of the **Holy Spirit;** consequently, we are not seeing the **finest anointing of God flow** as we read about in the Word of God.

Sometimes, I ask myself why some gatherings are still called **churches**? The more **appropriate name** should be what Jesus called them in **Revelation 2:9**.

This just dropped in my Spirit, but I have pondered on it before: **Jesus** in the **Gospel** is like an introduction to the **Son of God,** the **Messiah,** but in the **Book of Revelation**, it's like, "The honeymoon is over; don't hide behind **grace** and think you will get away with **evil** and **ignorance."**

I hundred percent believe that churches are **blocking the flow** of what God wants to do in these last days because other forces **not of God** are incorporated in the activities of some churches.

For the most part, I write about what I have experienced and what the Holy Spirit wants me to write.

God recently opened my eyes to something going on that **shocked me**—not necessarily the activity, but the people involved.

Some people would have never of heard about this **(evil altar).** The Bible says people suffer for lack of knowledge.

Some churches are **like** Sunday schools in what they preach, as these **churches have SOLD OUT** and **relinquished their authority.** I don't even need to mention to whom; you all know what's up.

My eyes were recently opened to a church that **erected an evil altar** so they could **transfer a person's glory, virtues and blessings** to someone else.

Now, I had **loads of dreams** about this person they were transferring it to, and I was wondering why I kept seeing this person in my dreams.

The Lord could have made it **crystal clear from day one**, which He did, but my **eyes were only open a little.** Just recently, He made my **eyes wide open**.

I do wonder how such folks sleep at night, because it is a **ridiculous, evil and dumb thing to do**.

As I have mentioned in the past, there are different types of souls. We have baby souls, infant souls, matured souls and old souls.

Old souls are also **masters**, but such person needs to **grow** into being a master in this **earthly realm.**

In as much as a person was sent as a master from the spirit realm before one was **formed in his mother's womb**, such a person's soul often needs to be afflicted to grow here on earth.

The reason I say this is because **if one is an old soul, there are things you would rather DIE than do because you are fully aware that ALL actions have heavenly/spiritual ramifications.**

Hence, to all those involved who have **aided and abetted** (I know most of you) in erecting the evil altar, to transfer one's blessing, glory and virtues, I have one question: **HOW DO YOU SLEEP AT NIGHT?**

The Lord says **Justice** and **Vengeance is His. He** will repay. I **BELIEVE** this, Lord.

The Lord took His time in making the incident **crystal-clear** to me, to teach me, to show me those involved, and to grow me.

Such **ungodly** activities affect the flow of God in a church and hinders us from seeing the **finest anointing**, which the Holy Spirit wants to pour out.

As I earlier mentioned some unclean spirits have entered churches, and it's affecting the flow of the Holy Spirit.

It's obvious how these unclean spirits came in, but I don't want to go into that. All that is happening in the Body today is written in the Bible.

There are many warning from our Lord Jesus, the apostles and from the Old Testament about following other gods and worshiping idols.

In **Acts 19, from verse 14,** the Bible says that when the Jews and Greeks living in Ephesus heard what had happened to the seven sons of Sceva, they were seized with fear.

We need the **FEAR of the Lord** back in the churches. I know it's getting darker and darker, but we have to take a stand and say **enough is enough.**

In v**erse 19, it says** that a number who had practiced sorcery brought their scrolls together and burned them publicly. When they calculated the value of the scrolls, the total came to fifty thousand drachmas.

Back then, all those who practiced dark magic, witchcraft and sorcery, brought their books together and burned them publicly.

In some **churches today,** the opposite is taking place. People are not burning the books; they are **using these doctrines of demons in church.**

This is simply the reason we struggle to see what God did with Apostle Paul. Let's take Acts 19 from the top.

Acts 19:1-7: "And it came to pass, that, while Apollos was at Corinth, Paul having passed through the upper coasts came to Ephesus: and finding certain disciples,

2 he said unto them, **Have ye received the Holy Ghost since ye believed?** And they said unto him, we have not so much as heard whether there be any Holy Ghost.

3 And he said unto them, unto what then were ye baptized? And they said, Unto John's baptism.

4 Then said Paul, John verily baptized with the baptism of repentance, saying unto the people, that they should believe on him which should come after him, that is, on Christ Jesus.

5 When they heard this, they were baptized in the name of the Lord Jesus.

6 And when Paul had laid his hands upon them, the Holy Ghost came on them; and they spoke with tongues, and prophesied.

7 And all the men were about twelve."

These disciples Apostle Paul found or came across in Ephesus were believers, like you and me. The apostle, in his wisdom, **knew the Holy Ghost** was **essential** to living the Christian life and to being effective.

Therefore, my question to the many churches we have all over the place is this: **has your congregation received the Holy Ghost since they believed**? If not, **WHY?** I didn't say have they received the kundalini spirit or a familiar spirit (spirits of demons). I said the **HOLY SPIRIT**.

If you are a minister of the Gospel, then you should be full of the Holy Spirit, and you should lay hands on people to receive the Holy Ghost. The Bible didn't say that the Apostle Paul preached them a sermon or offered them a leadership course or asked when or what Bible College or seminary they attended or will attend. He simply asked, "Have you received the **Holy Ghost?"**

In verse 6, it says, "When **Paul had laid his hands upon them, the Holy Ghost came on them; and they spoke with tongues, and prophesied."**

If all the money-making conferences were reduced a little, and if ministers used that time to be full of the Holy Ghost and to lay hands on their congregation, they would see the results Apostle Paul saw: people speaking in tongues and prophesying.

What I don't understand is why some Christian gatherings are more interested in people receiving the kundalini spirit or a familiar spirit.

I was in a church service some time ago, and someone laid hands on me and was praying. I couldn't hear what the person was praying, but when got home later, I felt something moving inside of me, and I asked Lord where it had come from. He told me, so I got on my knees and **prayed some warfare prayers and cast that sucker kundalini spirit out.**

A person can always know when a spirit other than the Holy Spirit is inside them. This can even happen when a person is **asleep;** the enemy could send evil spirits a person's way. They could put **something in your food**, and they could **use an object** or even a **simple handshake.**

Therefore, my advice to every serious believer is to have **POWER-FUL WARFARE PRAYERS** as part of one's praying tools.

Just being a Christian or even praying in the Holy Spirit alone WILL NOT always stop the enemy's attacks; one has to use **appropriate prayer points.**

This knowledge is from **experience**, not from a sermon or read from a book.

I have been watching some **street preachers lately on YouTube**. I want to give a shout-out for the **great job** they are doing. I am praying for these people, and they must make sure they are always prayed up. These guys are preaching more **truth** than most churches.

Street preaching is good, but if someone asks you to recommend a church to them, to be honest, it's hard to suggest one. Many churches are about numbers and money. Ministers preach **Jesus of the Gospel**, which is **excellent**, but they **NEVER preach Jesus of the Book of Revelations.**

Well, it is what it is; we are in the **last days Christianity**.

Acts 19:11 says that God continued to do extraordinary miracles through Paul. When **handkerchiefs and aprons that had touched his skin were taken to the sick, their diseases left them, and evil spirits went out of them**.

Can we just imagine that for a second? There was so much **anointing** on the great Man of God, using **ONLY** the Power of the **Holy Spirit**, and when handkerchiefs and aprons that had touched his skin were taken to the sick, they were healed, and evil spirits fled.

I believe the above verses 100 percent, and I totally believe that God can do it again and again and again. However, the **cost of the anointing is HIGH.**

The **cost** is **prayer, fasting, holiness**, and the **Word of God.** There will also be **spiritual attacks**.

No other POWER (apart from the mighty name of Jesus and the Holy Spirit) can **protect me** from the kingdom of darkness.

I have been experiencing spiritual warfare since I was a child. I have been around the block, and I can honestly say from my experience that God's power is more than enough for me. Sometimes it seems like the enemy is winning, but in the **twinkling of an eye,** the enemy that came **one way** has fled **seven ways**.

The power of God is so real to me that I could NEVER trade it for something else. The **sweetness of the anointing puts a smile on one's face.**

The anointing is so **pure and sweet,** just like a little child (I am talking of the sweetness of it). The other side is the **FIRE of the Holy Spirit,** that's when the **Holy Spirit is waging war and going to battle for us.**

The Holy Spirit is also **love.** The Bible says in **Romans 5:5** that the Love of God is shed in our hearts through the Holy Spirit.

The Holy Spirit also gives us a **glimpse of the New Heaven and the New EARTH.** I have nothing against money. Money is a handy tool, but **Money can't buy what the Holy Spirit gives, which the finest is anointing (the power of God).**

My wish would be that the **whole world** would have a **relationship** with the **Holy Spirit,** but that's just wishful thinking, I know.

CHAPTER 17

THE HOLY SPIRIT SHOWS US GOD'S MERCY WITH REPENTANCE

At this moment, I can't think of any better example that shows God mercy, which led to repentance, than that of one of my favorite characters of the New Testament.

I sometimes call him the **Great Apostle Paul**, because of what he endured, of how God used him in imaginable ways, and of the **wisdom and revelation** from his letter (epistles) which are the **core truths** that **most Christians** stand on today.

Apostle Paul didn't start this way. He persecuted the church after the death of Jesus.

However, God had a plan for him before the **foundation of the Earth, and he has a plan for you and for me.**

In **Roman's 2:4b**, it states that God's kindness is intended to lead a person to repentance.

God is rich in mercy, and when he shows us mercy, He gives power (the Holy Spirit) to turn **from darkness to light**.

On his road to Damascus, Apostle Paul encountered the Lord. This changed his life forever.

God's mercy goes hand in hand with repentance, but we can't turn from our old ways in **our strength.** We the **need the power of the Holy Spirit.**

In as much as we have to show mercy as God does, we also forgive. However, if the person in question is a **manipulator**, then it's advisable to **keep one's distance.** In other words, love them from a distance. As the saying goes, **once bitten twice shy**.

Apostle Paul stated that he received mercy because his actions were based on **ignorance and unbelief. (1 Timothy 1:13)**. However, the fact also remains that God had a calling on Apostle Paul from the onset.

When God is ready to get one's attention to fulfil one's divine destiny, nothing in the world can stop God.

As I began to think of God's mercy further, my mind went to one of the Old Testament favorites: King David, the man after God's heart. God's mercy always comes with repentance, but there is always a **consequence of our actions.**

If there is no repentance on our behalf, and if we keep on doing the same thing, then **I don't think God's mercy is available**

God's mercy always comes with remorse, but there is **still a consequence of our actions.**

King David was genuinely repentant when Prophet Nathan confronted him, and God showed King David mercy. However, if we look at both **Apostle Paul and King David, we see their actions didn't go totally without consequence.**

God can allow the consequences to be reduced, but it seems **we reap what we sow.**

We all know the story of King David and the troubles he faced after his terrible act.

Saul, whose name later changed to Paul, had a **harrowing life**. Thinking about it, it's God that gives us our ability; therefore, He could have given Apostle Paul's ability to any other apostle.

What I am wondering is, could any of the **pain Apostle Paul faced be due to his behavior when he was Saul,** such as his persecution of the Church and his role in Stephen's death?

God is rich in mercy when there is true repentance, but let's not rule out a reduced consequence for our actions, as **God cannot be mocked. We will reap what we sow.**

CHAPTER 18

THE HOLY SPIRIT REVEALS THE DEEPER REASON

We have heard the saying that there is more to life than meets the eye.

In **Deuteronomy 29:29,** the Word of God says, "The secret things belong unto the Lord our God, but the things which are revealed belong to us and our children forever, that we may do all of the words of this law."

Sometimes, or maybe most of the time, I want to know some of the secret things to make sense of what I see.

Apostle Paul's experience in **2 Corinthians 12.2b** "was caught up into Paradise and heard inexpressible words which man is not permitted to speak [words too sacred to tell]."

The classic Amplified version worded it a little differently: "caught up into Paradise, and he heard utterances **beyond the power of man** to put into **words**, which man is **not permitted to utter**."

There are still a lot of mysteries of the spiritual world, and to make sense of one's life, one has to go deeper.

In the Gospel of **Luke 7:28**, the Amplified Bible, Classic Edition (AMPC) states:

"I tell you, among those born of women there is no one greater than John; but he that is inferior [to the other citizens] in the kingdom of God is greater [in incomparable privilege] than he."

I believe that the **human soul** has **two purposes** on **Earth**:

The **first purpose**, which I think is the **primary reason**, is what I call a **heavenly spiritual purpose**.

The **second purpose** (secondary) is the **earthly spiritual purpose**, such as being **called** and **chosen** for a particular or specific reason **(a higher calling)**.

In the above verse, **Apostle Paul** said he heard utterances beyond the power of man to put into words. I believe that God allowed that incident to happen to let us know there are truths and mysteries in our spiritual journey that we are clueless about.

Jesus gave us a little hint in **Luke 7.28** when He said that no one born of man is greater than **John**, but he is the least in the **Kingdom of God**.

Could our primary **heavenly reason** for this spiritual journey have anything to do with **our position** in the **Kingdom of God**.?

According to Jesus in the above verse, different people have different, incomparable privileges in Paradise.

Apostle Paul mentioned "utterances beyond the power of man to put into words." Could this be part of the truth that some souls have an inner knowing that they are willing to lay down their lives instead of bowing down, such as the thee Hebrew boys (**Shadrach**, **Meshach**, and **Abednego**) and **Prophet Daniel** in the lion's den?

A lot of times, people know some **mysteries**, but it's beyond the power of man to put them into **words**.

I always ponder on the thought that, when I get **back home (Paradise)**, there will be things that will be revealed to my soul that I will say I knew all along when I was on my **pilgrimage**.

There are things that our **soul** knows but it is beyond the power of man to explain them. I often have naps, and I get the feeling my soul journeys to Heaven for instructions and refreshing, but I can't **prove it**.

In regard to the word **pilgrimage**, it's fair to say, **Jacob**, the **father of Joseph**, was very spiritual. One can know how spiritual or heavenly-minded a person is by how they **SPEAK** or **PREACH**

In **Genesis 47: 8-9**, Pharaoh asked Jacob his age:

And Pharaoh asked Jacob "How old are you?" 9 Jacob said to Pharaoh, "The years of my **pilgrimag**e are a hundred and thirty. Few and unpleasant have been the years of my life, and they have not reached the years that my fathers lived during the days of their **Pilgrimage**."

The word Jacob used, *pilgrimage*, means "a religious journey, a **holy expedition**."

An *expedition* is a journey undertaken by a group of people with a particular purpose.

Jacob started his journey with his brother **Esau**.

God later added to his journey, as one of the purposes was to create the **12 tribes of Israel** that we have today, and also part of the New Heaven and Earth.

In the **book of Hebrews**, it says we are **strangers** and **pilgrims** on the earth, but not everybody sees it that way. **People's actions** reveal what they know and understand.

In the **New Testament**, we are called the **Ambassadors of Christ**, which means we are **representing the Kingdom of God.**

God has His way of doing things, but He gives us **free will.** If you are **not part** of His Kingdom, please don't be **offended** by His **Divine Order**, as it **doesn't apply to you.**

Those who are **part of God's kingdom** are **willing to lay down their lives** rather than **bow down,** as we saw with **Shadrach**, **Meshach**, and **Abednego** and **Prophet Daniel** in the lion's den.

We are on a **pilgrimage**, and there is more to **life** than meets the **eye.**

CHAPTER 19

THE HOLY SPIRIT HELPS US CONTEND FOR OUR FAITH

The Holy Spirit gave me a vision, and I was to go to this place.

I didn't have a clue why and wanted to put it off till next week, but thank goodness I didn't. I was obedient, as I could have missed what God wanted to say.

This place was a church I have had visited before, nor did I know the name. I just knew the location and was familiar with the area, as my sister had lived near the neighborhood many years ago.

The area has changed a lot, and as I was approaching the location, I saw a lot of people of a different faith (Muslims). There were a couple of mosques in the area.

When I got to the destination, the name of the church was **St Gabriel**, and the service was to start in an hour and fifteen minutes.

I went for a drive, wondering why the Lord asked me to come to **St. Gabriel's Church.** It's typical of the Lord to ask his servants to go to a particular place where He speaks to them. This happens in the Bible, and it's common in the faith.

However, I still didn't know why He asked me to go to St Gabriel's Church. I later found out that today was Eid, a religious celebration for Muslims, which explained why I saw so many Muslims in their religious outfits.

To point out, I have nothing against people of different faiths—to each his own. I have come across people of different faiths, and some of them are brilliant people. **I am not an evangelist.**

When I got back to the church, I was observant, as I wanted to know the reason I was sent here and what the Lord wanted to say.

Before the service started, **I HEARD THE LORD SAY, "WE HAVE TO CONTEND FOR THE FAITH."** As I pondered on it, it all started to come together. Other religions take their faith more seriously than Christians, and they are growing in number.

As I googled "contend for the Faith," I found a verse in the **book of Jude.**

I also realised from an article by the Bible Project that the verse/text was used to refute **corrupt teachers/preachers** who lived **immoral lives.**

Let's have a look at **Jude 3 and 4:**

Beloved, while I was making every effort to write you about our common salvation, I was compelled to write to you [urgently] appealing that you fight strenuously/Contend for [the defense of] the Faith which was once for all handed down to the saints [the Faith that is the sum of Christian belief that was given verbally to believers].

4 **For certain people have crept in unnoticed [just as if they were sneaking in by a side door].** They are **ungodly** persons whose condemnation was predicted **long ago**, for they distort the grace of our God into decadence *and* immoral freedom [viewing it as an opportunity to do whatever they want], and deny *and* disown our only **Master and Lord, Jesus Christ.**

Putting all this together, the reason the Lord sent me to this particular area was to show me how this other religion takes their faith more seriously than us. Most of the people in this congregation were elderly; hence my question was, how come the **younger generation thinks they don't need God?**

Verse 4 in the Book of Jude says, "For certain people have crept in unnoticed." **God's DIVINE ORDER IS in His word.** Those who have crept into the Church (I don't need to mention who they are, as we all know them and the churches they control) are trying to change **God's divine order.**

Those who **crept** in will ultimately affect the faith, and God is saying we have to earnestly contend for the faith. God is going to judge the **pastors** who have **sold out** and severely **compromised**, unless they **repent.**

People were martyred and burned alive for the faith/Christianity. People that had the courage to translate the Bible into English (**like <u>William Tyndale</u>),** and **Martin Luther** risked his life during the Protestant Reformation for the liberty you and I **enjoy today.**

If this generation thinks they can **sell out** and bring another doctrine (the doctrine of demons)/**PREACH another Jesus** and believe/think they will go **SCOT-FREE,** sorry to **disappoint you, but you were taught wrong.**

WE MUST FOLLOW **GOD'S DIVINE ORDER.** He that hath an ear, let him hear what the Spirit says unto the churches (**Revelation 2:29).**

CHAPTER 20

THE HOLY SPIRIT SHOWS US GOD'S DIVINE ORDER. PART 1

Every country has a **constitution**, and its definition is a body of fundamental principles or established precedents according to which a state or other organization is acknowledged to be governed.

No president or prime minister is above the constitution of his or her country, as everybody will agree with this.

Now when it comes to God's Kingdom, our constitution is the **Word of God**, **Nobody** is above the **Word of God**.

What we see today is that, due to whatever reason, some members of God's Kingdom **cherry-pick** what to **obey** and what to **preach** from the Word of God.

The Bible says in **Romans 12:2,** "And do not be **conformed** to this world [any longer with its superficial values and customs], but be **transformed** *and* progressively changed [**as you mature spiritually**] by the renewing of your mind [**focusing on godly values and ethical attitudes**], so that you may prove [for yourselves] what the will of God is, that which is **good** and **acceptable and perfect** [in His plan and purpose for you]."

We, the Kingdom of God, **obey** the **rules and laws** of the **land**, but we **DO NOT** follow the Word's superficial values and customs. We go by what the Word of God says.

I know there are **sell-outs** in the body (which I don't consider them part of the body, but false and fake), and they are **bringing** the **world** into the **Church**, but we **rejec**t anything that is not of God in **Jesus' Name. Amen.**

Therefore, we must follow God's divine order, the constitution of the Kingdom of God, as we are in the **last days**, and we will have to give an **account** for our **lives**.

In every facet of life, we have orders set in place; in other words, there is a sequence to how things are done to achieve a desirable or perfect outcome.

The word **order** means "the arrangement or disposition of people or things concerning each other according to a particular sequence, pattern, or method."

It also **means** "an authoritative command or instruction."

In the political arena, there is order. The **UK** and the **USA**, both have democratically elected governments. The order of things in these two countries is slightly different, but there is still order in both political systems.

In the secular world, there are set ways of doing things. It's wise to understand the culture, but you don't have to conform to it.

What is acceptable in one country could be unacceptable in another, and the extreme case could even be **punished** by **death**.

The secular order of doing things is also different from the spiritual.

Again, we **obey** the laws of the land, but we don't have to **live** by any **secular** culture (we are not breaking the law).

There are **different** arms of government responsible for creating legislation and enforcing the law.

Having said the above, as it's in the **natural**, so it is in the **spiritual**.

The Holy Bible calls Christians **ambassadors** for **Christ**; in other words, we represent God's Kingdom (well, we should unless folks have sold out).

As we have order in this natural, we also have order in the spiritual world.

There is order in the spirit world in both kingdoms the Kingdom of **Light** and the kingdom of **darkness**.

It's essential that we **distinguish** between the two, as we know some churches preach differently from the Bible and from what **Apostle Paul** and the other **apostles** taught.

In a **civilized society**, no one imposes their beliefs on another, but it's **crucial** that one **stands** for something or one would **fall** for everything.

A **Christian** is in this world, **but** not of it.

The god of this **world** is the devil, and he has his **system** in place.

It is important one knows the difference; that's why, as Christians, we have to understand what the Word of God says.

Usually, the devil's ways are **opposite** to God's ways; we call his ways **abominations**.

The good thing is we live in a **free society**, so we choose what we believe and who we follow. God has given us **free will.**

Who does the secular world follow? In terms of principles, for the most part, it would be the **god** of this world. (the **fallen archange**l himself).

Some of the people who follow the god of this world are **nice people**; spiritually, they don't know any **better.**

On the **other hand**, some people who follow the god of this world are **agents** of the kingdom of **darkness**, so you must watch your back.

THE HOLY SPIRIT SHOWS US GOD'S DIVINE ORDER. PART 2

God's divine order has nothing to do with my **opinion**; it's what's written in the **Holy Bible**.

Since a **Christian** should have the **Holy Spirit** in them, they wouldn't fight the **leading** of the **Holy Spirit.** Unfortunately, you and I know not all who profess to be Christians have the **Holy Spirit** in them, and I believe that is a big problem.

We (**humans**) are all controlled by a **higher force**; the Holy Spirit should control a Christian. Some people are controlled by the **spirit of the world,** the **spirit of disobedience,** or **demons.**

The **divine order** of God will bear witness with our spirit, as Christians.

Let's start from the **beginning** of the Book (it's always the best place to start) and identify God's divine order.

God created **Adam**; **Eve** was then created from one of **Adam's ribs** to be **Adam's companion.**

As God said in **Genesis 2:18,** "Now the **Lord God** said, 'It is not good (beneficial) for the man to be alone; I will make him a helper [one who **balances him**—a counterpart who is] **suitable** *and* **complementary** for him.'"

Genesis 2:20b -24 says, "There was not found a helper [that was] suitable (a companion) for him. 21 So the **Lord God** caused a **deep sleep** to fall upon Adam; and while he slept, He took one of his ribs and closed up the flesh at that place. 22 And the rib which the Lord God had taken from the man He made (fashioned, formed) into a woman, and He brought her *and* presented her to the man. 23 Then Adam said,

'This is now bone of my bones,

And flesh of my flesh;

She shall be called **Woman**,

Because she was taken out of **Man**.'

24 For this reason a man shall leave his father and his mother, and shall be joined to his wife; and they shall become **one flesh**."

From the above, we can all agree that **God's Divine Order** is for man and woman to come together as one flesh, written in the Word of God, the constitution of the Heavenly Kingdom. **Amen**.

There will always be a **vacuum (a state of emptiness; a void)** in every human. Ideally, it would great if this state of emptiness were filled up by the **Holy Spirit**, but you and I know this not the case in our world, as most people like to live as they please without any **constraints (limitation or restriction).**

If a person wants to live without any constraints, they will find it hard to **honor God** and to have a **relationship with God**. Such people might still be **fascinated by supernatural** and **consequently** open themselves up to **dark and unclean spirits (demons).**

These unclean spirits (fallen angels) have the power to **change the dynamics** of a person, such as **sexual orientation**. The kingdom of darkness does this all the time. A lot of people attracted to the same sex have had their **natural sexual orientation altered** by the kingdom of **darkness.**

When we honor God, we want to please Him and live by His divine order, on the flip side people for those who don't honor God, according to **Apostle Paul** in **Romans1:26 -27**, the following happens. Here it is in the Amplified version.

For this reason **God** gave them over to **degrading *and* vile passions**; for their women exchanged the natural function for that which is unnatural [a function contrary to nature], 27 and in the same way also the men turned away from the natural function of the Woman and were consumed with their desire toward one another, men with men **committing shameful** acts and in return receiving in their own bodies the inevitable *and* **appropriate penalty for their wrongdoing.**

In summary, God **ordained** for **man** and **woman** to become one flesh; this is the **divine order of God**. The Word of God should be **respected** by the Body of Christ, as it seems some **Christians are confused** in this area, or maybe they have **sold out** and are doing what is **required** of them to do and say (you can't **fool** us).

THE HOLY SPIRIT SHOWS US GOD'S DIVINE ORDER. PART 3

A lot of religious folks like to cherry-pick when it comes to what they preach in church and how they conduct their services.

For people who are new to the faith, this could affect their foundation and harm their faith, as they would lack the knowledge of the ways of God.

It is common practice in some denominations to preach from certain parts of the Bible, depending on the doctrine they teach.

I know that ultimately, it's the responsibility of each person to know the Word of God, but churches also have a greater responsibility to be hundred-percent faithful to the Word of God.

I must say the faith has come a long way. To serve God, one must be bold and courageous, like **Martin Luther**. Martin Luther was a German monk who began the **Protestant Reformation** in the 16th century. He became one of the most influential and controversial figures in the history of <u>Christianity</u>.

There was a time in history when Christians were not allowed to read the Bible. They had to depend on the Church (to know God), which was the Catholic Church at the time. That's why we Christians will be forever grateful for the work of **William Tyndale.**

According to Tyndale, the Church <u>forbade owning or reading the Bible</u> to control and restrict the teachings and to enhance their own power and importance (Huff Post).

To faithfully serve God, one has to be a rebel and be radical to the establishment. One must also have zeal, we see these qualities in the lives of our **Saviour Jesus Christ**, **Apostle Paul**, **Martin Luther** and **William Tyndale,** to name but a few.

For the most part, **establishments are corrupt**; they **deceive people** and only care about themselves.

In God's divine order, I want to address what comes from the **Ten Commandments.** The **second** of the Ten Commandments is in the book of **Exodus 20: 4-6.**

4 You shall not make yourself any graven image [to worship it], or any likeness of anything that is in the heavens above, or that is in the earth beneath, or that is in the water under the earth;

5 You shall not bow down yourself to them or serve them; for I the Lord your God am a jealous God, visiting the iniquity of the fathers upon the children to the third and fourth generation of those who hate Me,

6 But showing mercy *and* steadfast love to a thousand generations of those who love Me and keep My commandments.

......

My question is, why does the **Catholic Church** and some of the **Churches of England** still have **statutes of Mary** and other **so-called saints** in their church in which people say **prayers to, bow down to** and **light candles ?**

I have prayed in front of statutes in the Catholic Church, as I went to a Catholic secondary school, so I have Catholic roots in me, but if one does their **homework**, the **Bible completely forbids it.**

Here are some verses to help us with what God says about idolatry

Psalm 97.7a (Amplified): "Let all those be [deeply] ashamed who serve carved images."

Deuteronomy 4:23-24: "Be careful not to forget the covenant of the LORD your God that he made with you; do not make for yourselves an idol in the form of anything the LORD your God has forbidden. For the LORD, your God is a consuming fire, a jealous God."

Deuteronomy 4:16-18: "So that you do not act corruptly and make a graven image for yourselves in the form of any figure, the likeness of male or female…"

Leviticus 26:1: "Do not make idols or set up carved images, or sacred pillars, or sculptured stones in your land so you may worship them. I am the LORD your God.

Therefore, **graven images** and **statues** are **not of God;** hence, any church that has them is **misleading the people.**

In **Psalm 103:7**, the Bible says, "He made known His ways [of righteousness and justice] to Moses, His acts to the Children of Israel."

As a Christian, if we are serious about getting closer to God, then our aim should be like that of **Moses:** to know **God's way.**

Finally, part of the creed in some **Churches of England** says they believe in the Catholic Church, but how can you believe in the **Catholic Church** when you don't follow a lot of the **Bible?**

Our **Lord** and **Saviour** put it this way in the **Gospel of John 4:23:** "But a time is coming and is already here when the true worshipers will worship the Father in spirit [from the heart, the inner self] and in truth; for the Father seeks such people to be His worshipers."

So, my fellow Christians, let's **follow John 4:23**, and worship **God** in **Spirit** and **truth.**

THE HOLY SPIRIT SHOWS US GOD'S DIVINE ORDER. PART 4

It's a great honor to serve God, but a lot of folks love the fancy titles more than preaching the truth; however, the person who teaches or preaches the Word of God will face a **stricter judgment**.

In **Acts 20: 19,** Apostle Paul had this to say on His way to Jerusalem: "Serving the Lord with all humility in tears and in the midst of adversity (affliction and trials) which befell me, due to the plots of the Jews [against me]." Some ministers/Christians **can't** relate to **Apostles Paul's pain** and some ministers **can**.

Apostle Paul often boasts of his pain and suffering in serving the Lord; today, ministers boast of the **resources** they have **accumulated** from preaching the **Word of God**. In the same chapter, **Apostle Paul** goes on to say this in **verses 26-27**:

Therefore I testify *and* protest to you on this [our parting] day that I am **clean** *and* **innocen**t *and* **not** responsible for the **blood** of any of you.

27 For I never shrank *or* kept back *or* fell short from declaring to you the whole purpose *and* plan *and* Counsel of God.

I want to **zero in on** some keywords in the above verses, the first is, he said, he was **NOT** responsible for the **blood** of any of you.

If a minister or preacher does not warn the **people** or **congregation** of their sin, and if the minister does not preach the **full Word of God**, and the people **perish,** then the **blood** of the people is on the minister.

Also, in **Ezekiel 3:18**, God says the following, "If I say to the **wicked**, You shall surely die, and you do not give him warning or speak to warn the wicked to turn from his wicked way, to save his life, the same wicked man shall die in his iniquity, but his **blood** will I require **at your hand.**"

To all the **seeker-friendly preachers,** those **preaching another gospel**, and churches that **pray to statues,** I have said what God has told me to say, and I do not have anyone's **blood on my hand.**

This stuff (the Word of God) is **serious;** we have to **repent.** Money brings comfort in this world, but you are not taking it with you. Your wealth will not be with you in the Day of Judgement. **Jeffery Epstein** didn't take his money with him, and his **end** was **not good.**

Ministers **who** manipulate the congregation out of money will have to **give an account** for it on that **day.** There is no teaching of Jesus or of the apostles that condones this.

The other part that the **Holy Spirit** I am **zeroing in on** is Acts 20:27 27: "For I **never shrank** *or* kept back *or* fell short from declaring to you the whole purpose *and* plan *and* **counsel of God.**"

Another word for counsel is **guidance**, direction, instruction, information, and **enlightenmen**t. Therefore, ministers are responsible to preach the full Word of God after **rightly dividing it.**

Allowing the congregation to **pray, to bow down** to and to **light candles** to **statues,** means the minister has shrunk or kept back or fell short from declaring to the congregation the whole purpose, plan and **counsel** of God, and according to Apostle Paul, **blood** could be on their **hands**.

When a person **truly preaches** the Word of God, there **MUST** be afflictions and persecution. It comes with **teaching** the **truth.**

Therefore, if there are no **persecutions,** I would question the **validity** of such a m**inister** and their **ministry.**

THE HOLY SPIRIT SHOWS US GOD'S DIVINE ORDER. PART 5

The **world** keeps on changing and **evolving**, and in the natural, it's advisable to **keep up** with the **times**.

However, with **spiritual issues (Christianity)**, one has to be very careful, as there is **no time** in the **spirit**.

Malachi 3:6a, says, "For I am the Lord, I **do no**t change."

Hebrews 13:8 says, "**Jesus** is the same **yesterday, today** and **forever**."

We can establish that in as much as the world **evolves,** the **Creator** of the universe **does no**t, God remains **constant.**

In today's world of **Christianity**, we all know that cherry-picking the Word of God is a **common theme.**

However, the **Bible warns** us in **Proverbs 14:12** that there is a way that seems right to a man and appears straight before him, but in the end, it is the **way of death.**

Many times with **spiritual stuff**, we don't immediately see the **impact** and **consequence** of us not fully following the **Word** of God.

The consequences of not obeying the Word of God could **take years** or even **generations.**

When God tells us to follow **specific patterns**, there are reasons **behind it**, and mostly we can't **comprehend them.**

Isaiah 55:8 says, "For **My thoughts** are not your thoughts, neither are your ways **My ways** says the Lord."

Verse 9 says, "For as the **heavens** are **higher** than the **earth**, so are **My ways higher** than your ways and **My thoughts** than your thoughts".

We **humans** cannot **outsmart** our **Creator**; often, we can't **grasp God's wisdom**. I would say it's best to put one's life on the line than be influenced by the **Babylonian** system as **compared** to the Word of God.

The above reminds me of a saying I heard some time ago: **God's Word** doesn't make **sense**; it makes **faith**.

We have seen so much **change** in our **world** and **society.** Years ago, things we see happening today would have been **unacceptable**, but as they say, we are in the last days. The **intolerable** has now become **acceptable**.

The world is **working** on creating a **new world order**, which is not my **prerogative,** as **I am in** the world but **not of it.**

God likes to **remind** us of His **divine order**, so we started from the Book of **Genesis**, and we saw how God created and formed **Adam and Eve.**

We see **God's pattern** for human creation and **relationships.** This is for people who **fear** and **reverence** the **Lord** our **God,** and for whom **Jesus Christ** is **Lord** and **Saviour.** It's not for everyone (it can be, but we all have **free will,** so you **decide** whom you want to **serve**).

Then we looked at the **second commandment** where God says do not **worship idols, statues** or pray in front of them, as our Lord **Jesus paid** the **price** so we can come to **God directly** in **Jesus' name.** Amen.

The Bible says to come **boldly** to the throne of grace where we find mercy and grace in our time of need. **Hebrews 4:16 says,** "Jesus took His last breath and said, **it is finished.**" Hence you and I can go into God's presence in **Jesus' name.** Amen.

The **next divine order** will be left for people to **reason it out** and to ask themselves why they chose to **disobey** this verse of **scripture**.

It may come across as **controversial**. Therefore, I am NOT going to **comment** much about it, and I will **just lay it out**.

1 Timothy 2: 11-15 (Amplified)

11. Let a woman learn in quietness, in entire submissiveness.

12 I allow no **woman to teach** or to have **authority over men**; she is to remain in quietness *and* keep silence [in religious assemblies].

13 For Adam was first formed, then Eve;

14 And it was **not Adam who was deceived**, but [the] **woman** who was **deceived** *and* deluded and **fell** into **transgression**.

15 Nevertheless [the sentence put upon women of pain in motherhood does not hinder their souls' salvation, and] they will be saved [eternally] if they continue in Faith and love and holiness with self-control, [saved indeed] through the Childbearing *or* by the birth of the divine Child.

We also see the same command in **1 Corinthians 14: 34-37** (amplified):

The women should **keep quiet** in the churches, for they **are not authorized** to speak, but should take a secondary *and* subordinate place, just as **the Law also says.**

35 But if there is anything they want to learn, they should ask their own husbands at home, for it is disgraceful for a woman to talk in church for her to **usurp and exercise authority over men in the church**].

36 What! Did the word of the Lord **originate with you** [Corinthians], or has it reached only you?

37 If anyone **thinks *and* claims that he is a prophet** [filled with and governed by the **Holy Spirit of God** and inspired to interpret the divine

will and purpose in preaching or teaching] or has any other spiritual endowment, let him understand (recognize and acknowledge) that what I am writing to you **is a command of the Lord.**

I will zero in on verse 37: "If anyone thinks and claims that he is a prophet or has any other spiritual endowment, let him understand that what I am writing to you **is a command of the Lord."**

My take on this is, I do believe what Apostle Paul wrote is a **command** of the **Lord**, and on a personal level, I have been **truly blessed** by **many female preachers,** and in fact, the most significant **spiritual gift** (**praying in the spirit**) the Lord blessed me with came with the help of a **female minister's ministry.**

Deborah, a female, was a **judge and prophetess** in the **Old Testament, but** God **was speaking** through His **servant Apostle Paul** in the **New Testament.**

So, I have **nothing against** female preachers, and they have their place among the **female believers.**

I **certainly** would **not feel** comfortable if a **female preacher** was the **senior pastor** of a church I attended.

In as much as she probably does an **excellent job**, the Word of the Lord would we be **ringing** in my **ear**, and this would keep / stop me **from receiving.**

This issue has nothing to do with ability or anointing; it's just **God's divine order.**

Remember, **Jesus Christ** is the **Light** and **Saviour** of the **world.**

THE HOLY SPIRIT SHOWS US GOD'S DIVINE ORDER, PART 6

This **divine order** I am going to write about is so **important** to the Christian faith.

It has **turned** unbelievers away from even wanting to have anything to do with the **faith**.

Also, for a lot of believers, it has **shipwrecked** their **faith**.

This divine order is called **MONEY.**

We have a brand of Christianity called **prosperity Gospel.**

From my observation, particular churches are big on **tithes** and offerings. Some churches such as the **Catholic Church** and the **Church of England (the Anglican Church)** only ask for an offering.

What is a **tithe**? A tithe is one-tenth of annual produce or earnings, formerly taken as a tax for the support of the church and clergy.

There is a lot about the tithe in the **Old Testament**. Now we are under the New Testament; therefore, technically it doesn't apply, and I like to believe that's the reason why the **Catholic and Anglican Church** don't ask for it or use that term.

I don't see the **tithe as a law** but as a **spiritual principle.** When you **give,** you **receive**. The spiritual **significance** of the tithe still applies, and **I believe** in it.

The question is, if you choose to give a tenth of your earnings away, who do you give it to? Technically, you could give it to the church that is **feeding** you **spiritually.**

However, what if a church is not really feeding you spiritually? In that case, you can give the tithe to a **charity**, an **orphanage**, **sponsor a child** from a developing country, etc.

A lot of unbelievers have seen **Christian television**, and it seems most of them are **hustling** for your **money**, and, the whole emphasis is about **giving** to the extent that you ask yourself, do I have to **pay** for a **blessing**?

Some churches preach the right message on God's blessing, and then after the message, they ask you to **sow a seed to receive the blessing** of the Word just **preached**.

A lot of **prosperity teaching** is around giving; basically, you give and get blessed. A lot of their teaching can be **backed up** with **scriptures**, which I am going to write down shortly, so one **could say** there is nothing wrong with it.

I believe it's essential that Christians know the **spiritual principle** involving our life, including money, but the **preaching of money** should be **secondary** and not the **core message** of Christianity.

People have seen, in many instances that **prosperity preachers** get **rich** from **taking the money** of the members of the **congregation**.

As a Christian, we **believe** everything we have comes from God, including what we earn, and to give a tenth of it away is **merely** doing **God's work.**

So, if you choose to give your tithe to an **orphanage** or to a **church** that feeds you **spiritually**, one is technically helping other people's needs in which they would have **prayed to God** about.

The Bible says God blesses us to be a blessing **(Genesis 12.2).**

In as much as **Jesus and Apostle Paul** did not teach on **tithing**, they both taught on **giving**. Let's see some of their teachings:

Luke, 6.38, Amplified.

Give, and [gifts] will be given to you; **good measure**, pressed down, shaken together, and running over, will they pour into [the pouch formed by] the bosom [of your robe and used as a bag]. For with the **measure** you deal out [with the measure you use when you confer **benefits** on others], it will be **measured back to you.**

Some people have the **natural gift** to be **generous.** We will reap what we sow, and sometimes, a person's generosity could invoke a blessing on the giver's **children**, for example, or on **future generations**.

So, Jesus is saying to give, and you will get more back. Looking at the above verse, it's not **limited to the Church** nor does it have to be the **Church**.

Matthew 6.3-4

But when you **give** to the **poor** *and* do acts of kindness, do not let your left hand know what your right hand is doing [give in complete secrecy], 4 so that your charitable acts will be done in secret; and your Father who sees [what is done] in secret will **reward** you

Again, reading the above verse, **God rewards** us when we **help Him out** by **giving** to the poor. Jesus taught spiritual **principles.**

One has **to come** to the place of **understanding** that Christianity is about learning and understanding **spiritual laws and principles**, just like we have laws from science such as the law of **gravity.**

Apostle Paul gave us the following giving principles:

2 Corinthians 9:7 Amplified

Let each one **give** [**thoughtfully and with purpose**] just as he has decided in his heart, **not grudgingly or under compulsion**, for God loves a cheerful giver [and delights in the one whose heart is in his gift].

According to the above verse, we should **not be manipulated** or **hypnotized** into **giving,** as this happens in some churches. The false and fake preachers see the House of God as a **business** and they look for ways to make **money** from the people.

It's a good practice to be **generous** and to be a **giving person.** As we help others, we are doing God's work, and He will reward the giver. We **don't technically give to get back**; it's just a spiritual principle and law, that as we give, the **blessing comes back**.

Prosperity is in the **Bible**, so I am not **knocking it**; however, it should be **secondary**, not the **primary preaching** of a church.

It is a **good thing** to be **successful** and **prosperous**, and to do so, I would say find your **passion** and put your **heart and soul** into it.

Once you have **found** your **passion**, create a **vision**. Talking about being a **visionary**, I would like to say that **Richard Williams** is one of the **greatest visionaries** of all times.

As a female tennis fan myself, I see how many other parents around the world have emulated the **vision/model** he had for his daughters (**Venus and Serena**) for their children.

Naomi Osaka's father probably emulated what **Richard Williams** did, and we saw the outcome.

THE HOLY SPIRIT SHOWS US GOD'S DIVINE ORDER, PART 7

To **flow** in **God's power**, we have to live **according** to His **divine order**.

There is something about **power** that humans **crave.** We know there are different **types** of power: **money power, physical power,** and **military power. America** prides itself on being the **most powerful country in the world.**

What I find **hilarious** is that countries with **power** try and stop other countries from **getting power.** (I won't get involved in **politics.** I don't think it's my **calling.**)

The **only power** I know is from **my helper.** Some call Him the **Holy Ghost,** and some call Him the **Holy Spiri**t. I call Him both of the above, but **He** also is my **best friend.**

I **can't survive** without His **power.**

However, there are **conditions** to the *Holy Ghost power:* one **MUST** live by the Holy Word of God (*God's divine order*).

The main reason I do my best to live according to God's divine order is that I need His Power.

I have a lot of enemies. Everywhere I go, they show up. **It's not if;** it's **when and how.** Therefore, I need Holy Ghost power to **discern** what they are up to. When they come against me, **I MUST be ready** to fight the good fight of faith, which we call *spiritual warfare*.

There are some things my **flesh wants**. Hence, I have to put my **flesh** in **check** and let my **spirit** have and take **dominion**.

13 For if you **live** according to [**the dictates of**] the flesh, you will **surely die**. But if through the **Power of the [Holy] Spirit** you are [habitually] **putting to death** (making extinct, deadening) the [evil] deeds prompted by the body, you shall [really and genuinely] live forever. (**Romans 8:13 Amplified Bible**)

If the enemy already has you, **he doesn't fight you**. If the enemy doesn't have **control** over you, then he fights you everywhere you go, so that's the story of my life. I am an **old soul**, so I'll be **alright**. My eyes are on the **eternal** weight of **glory**.

The **Bible** says be **vigilan**t and **watchful.** Nowadays, we need eyes all around our head. In spiritual terms, our **discernment** must be **strong**.

The Bible says:

8 Be well balanced (temperate, sober of mind), be vigilant *and* cautious at all times; for that enemy of yours, the devil, roams around like a lion roaring in fierce hunger], seeking someone to seize upon *and* devour. (**1 Peter 5:8**)

That's why one can't afford not to live by God's divine order, as we live by God's word. Not only does it give us confidence that we will win the battle; it provides us faith that we can hear God clearly.

Some folks say we don't live by emotion but by faith, which is true, but faith works alongside with peace and peace is an emotion.

According to hopefaithprayer.com, **peace** is the **emotion of faith**. Peace is that condition of the **heart that communicates** to us that **God is fully** involved in our situation.

Yes, we **live by faith** not by sight (2 Corinthians 5:6b), and when God is in it, He backs it up with the **assurance of PEACE.**

Therefore, if in doubt, don't move and **continue** to **seek God.** If there is no peace about a situation, put it on hold. Trust me, **there is good reason to wait.**

Like the lyrics of the song by **Sarah Reeves to "I Just Want You,"** if **God's not in it, I don't want it**, and if God's not in it, there will be no peace about it.

In fact, our **prayer** should be, "If **You** are **not in any action** I want to take, may it never happen and may I have **no peace about it."**

Let us never **underestimate** the **power of peace.** The **Bible says:**

7 and the Peace of God, which surpasses all understanding, will guard your hearts and minds through Christ Jesus. **Philippians 4:7** New King James Version (NKJV)

The **amplified version** puts it this way, "And God's Peace [shall be yours, that [a]tranquil state of a soul assured of its salvation through Christ, and so fearing nothing from God and being content with its earthly lot of whatever sort that is, that Peace] which transcends all understanding shall [b]garrison *and* mount guard over your hearts and minds in Christ Jesus."

When one is full of the precious Holy Ghost, its **obvious** and **conspicuous**, but more importantly, it provides a **state of tranquillity.** The **Holy Ghost** is the answer to the **mental health issues** that are so **rampant these days.**

In the **early Church,** such a **term** never existed; all they knew was that **God** had given them a **spirit of POWER, LOVE and a SOUND MIND.**

My **heart goes out** to the people who **suffer with mental health, especially** in the **body of Christ.** However, there is a **big problem here:** the **members** of the **congregation.**

If a **pastor** takes his life, who is meant to be the **pillar of the Faith and strength,** it's an **important issue** that **Church leaders** need to **address**, as it doesn't help **contend for the faith.**

Again, my **heart** and **prayers** go out to the **loved ones** and **families** who have **lost** someone due to **mental health issues.**

I also believe there is something **terribly wrong** in the **Christian faith protocol**, and it needs to **be addressed.** Many of their practices are nowhere found in the **Bible.** Please don't forget, everybody will account for their actions.

Such a **protocol** involves **much manipulation**, and this **hinders God's plan**. The good thing with **God** is that He always has **many other options.**

Preachers should **cut out the games** and **keep it real.** People are not stupid. When games are being played, **people realize it**, and it **causes mistrust.**

I **wonder** what percentage of people **don't trust preachers.** We all need the **power** of the **Holy Spirit** to **endure** to the **end, especially the body of Christ.** Mechanical religion will **not cut it.**

THE HOLY SPIRIT SHOWS US GOD'S DIVINE ORDER, PART 8

For the Holy Spirit to communicate God's divine order to us requires an essential task from our part.

This undertaking, called **prayer**, has been removed from most **schools**. In a lot of instances, it has been done away with in many **churches**.

Psalm 109, verse 4b says, "**But I gave myself to prayer.**" Prayer is the only way to see the incomparable power of a Christian at work.

In these last days, with the world getting **darker** and **darker**, the **ONLY** way to survive is to give ourselves to **prayer**.

Corporate prayer is **excellent** and has its **place**, as it brings our attention to the importance of Prayer, but if you are a **target**, or if you are **marked** by the **enemy,** the only way to **overcome** is to **give yourself to personal prayer**, alone with **God**.

As an **introvert,** my best way to **pray** is **alone.** The **enemy** can **strike** at any time; hence, one has to be ever **ready** to **engage** in the **authority** given by our Saviour and to use it for whatever **battle** comes one's way.

In fact, what I have seen in the last several years has made me conclude that **prayer is not only a lifestyle for a Christian** but **spiritual warfare** is also a **way of life, especially** for those who are **targets** of the **enemy**.

It is in **prayer** that we have the **mind of Christ**. The Bible says in **1 Corinthians 2:16,** "For who has known the **mind *and* purposes of the Lord**, so as to instruct Him? But we have the mind of Christ [to be guided by His **thoughts** and **purposes**]."

The above verse can also be linked to **Romans 8: 26-28.** The Holy Spirit helps us in prayer, so that we know **God's purpose,** and in this **engagement**, we have the **mind of Christ.**

Romans 8- 26-28: "In the same way, the Spirit [comes to us and] helps us in our weakness. We do not know what prayer to offer *or* how to offer it as we should, but the Spirit Himself [knows our need and at the right time] intercedes on our behalf with sighs *and* groanings too deep for words. 27 And He who searches the hearts knows what the mind of the Spirit is, because the Spirit intercedes [before God] on behalf of [a] God's people in accordance with God's will.

28 And we know [**with great confidence**] that God [**who is deeply concerned about us**] causes all things to work together [as a plan] for good for those who love God, to those who are **called according to His plan *and* purpose.**"

If you have been **walking with the Lord** for a while, you will have realized that **God's purpose** is not as **straightforward** as we would like it to be. In fact, there often seems to be a lot of **confusion in the atmosphere.**

What we have to be fully aware of is that **God is not the author of confusion (2 Corinthians 14:33).** It's the enemy of our soul and his agents that put us in a state of puzzlement; hence, **prayer is critical.**

No human being can **genuinely and effectively serve God** without prayer; it's only the **false and fake ministers who don't need prayer.** Any church that **does not emphasize** the importance of prayer is a church **one MUST flee.**

Whatever **God** is leading a person to fulfill as their **spiritual assignment**, there will be **opposition. (2 Corinthians16:9)** For a great door and effectual is opened unto me, and there are many adversaries.

Therefore, we have to be **good soldiers** and **carry on with our work**.

Prayer equals POWER; there is no shortcut.

The prayers of the **early Church** enabled them to spread the **Good News of Jesus Christ,** which you and I benefit from today.

It's when we pray that we will have power, so the world can see the **manifestations** of **the sons/daughters of God. Romans 8:19:** "For [even the whole] creation [all nature] waits eagerly for the **children of God** to be revealed."

It is also when we pray that we will be people who know their God and be **strong and do exploits. (Daniel 11:32 Amplified),** but the people who [are **spiritually mature** and] **know their God** will display **strength** and take **action [to resist]**.

It is from **prayer** that we can **boldly** share our faith and **not be** intimidated by anyone.

CHAPTER 21

THE HOLY SPIRIT GIVES GIFTS

In **Matthew17:21**, when the disciples couldn't cast the demon out of the demoniac boy, Jesus came to their rescue. They asked Jesus why they couldn't **cast the demon out of the boy. Jesus replied** that this type comes out by **praying and fasting**. (I recently heard that *fasting* wasn't part of the original text; it was added later).

Another way of putting what Jesus said is to say there are **different levels of POWER** for **various tasks**. We know that **praying and fasting equal POWER.**

Therefore the disciples **did not have enough Power to get the job done**. If we want to have **dominion in this dark world**, we have to get on our knees and PRAY, because **PRAYER EQUALS POWER. AMEN.**

The prophet Isaiah said in the Book of Isaiah, **Chapter 41, verse 11** that those who **strive** with you shall **PERISH.**

Strive means struggle or fight vigorously (e.g., those who use dark magic on a Christian)

Perish means die, especially in a violent or sudden way.

The words of **Prophet Isaiah** align with **Psalm 105:15,** "Do not touch My **anointed ones** and do my Prophets **no harm.**

Anointing means the **Power of God**; therefore, if the Power of God is active on any of His servants and if people use **demonic power** or **witchcraft** on an individual, they are doing it **at their own risk.**

As Jesus said, **this situation** (the demoniac boy) **requires more power** to cast the demon out; likewise, if an **anointed servant of God** has **sufficient power** on them at the **time of the attack**, the **perpetrator,** according to **Prophet Isaiah, would PERISH.**

Power in prayer comes from **praying the scriptures** (God's promises) as **God's Word cannot and will not return void**; the second type of praying is **praying in the Holy Spirit.**

It is **fair to say** when we **pray** in the **Holy Spirit,** the **gifts of the Holy Spirit** are coming on us. We know that the **gift of faith** comes on us, as in the book of **Jude 20** Amplified Bible (AMP):

20 But you, beloved, build yourselves up on [the foundation of] your most holy Faith [continually progress, **rise like an edifice higher and higher**], **pray in the Holy Spirit.**

However, when we are praying in the Holy Spirit, we should earnestly desire *and* cultivate the spiritual *gifts* [to be used by believers for the benefit of the church], **1 Corinthians 14.1b.** Let's define some **keywords** here:

Earnestly means seriously.

Desire means a strong feeling of wanting to have something or wishing for something to happen. Without passion in life, for the most part, we don't get anything.

Cultivate means to acquire or develop a skill.

In other words, we have to put a **demand on the power of God**, and as **FAITHFUL as God is,** He will give it to us for **one purpose only**: to be a **blessing to His Church**, because He will build His Church and the gates of Hell WILL **NOT prevail** against it. **Amen.**

Let's have a look at the **various gifts** mentioned by **Apostle Paul.**

1 Corinthians 12: 8-10.

To one is given through the [Holy] Spirit [the Power to speak] the message of wisdom, and to another [the power to express] the word of knowledge *and* understanding according to the same Spirit; 9 to another [wonder-working] faith [is given] by the same [Holy] Spirit, and to another the [extraordinary] gifts of healings by the one Spirit; 10 and to another the working of [a]miracles, and to another prophecy [foretelling the future, speaking a new message from God to the people], and to another discernment of spirits [the ability to distinguish sound, godly doctrine from the deceptive doctrine of man-made religions and cults], to another *various* kinds of [unknown] tongues, and to another interpretation of tongues.

According to the above **scripture**, we have the **following gifts:**

1. Gift of wisdom

2. Gift of the word of knowledge and understanding

3. Gift of faith

4. Gift of healing

5. Gift of miracles

6. Gift of prophecy

7. Gift of discerning of spirits

8. Gift of tongues

9. Gift of interpretation of tongues

Again, according to Apostle Paul, we should **desire** the **above spiritual gifts.**

I **wonder** whether a person could **operate and flow** in **all the gifts** of the **Holy Spirit.** Based on the Word of God, we can. I believe a person can walk in **all the gifts of the Holy Spirit.**

Looking at **Jesus' ministry**, it's fair to say that **Jesus had all the gifts** of the **Holy Spirit in operation,** and we can name each of these gifts in various situations in **His three years of ministry.**

We also have to remember what **Jesus** said in **John 14: 12-13** (Amplified):

12 I assure you *and* most solemnly say to you, anyone who believes in Me [as Savior] will also do the things that I do; and he will do even greater things than these [in extent and outreach] because I am going to the Father. 13 And I will do whatever you ask in My name [as My representative], this I will do, so that the Father may be glorified *and* celebrated in the Son.

In the above verse, **Jesus said that whatever** we ask in His name to **help build His Church** He will give it to us.

In summary, we should **earnestly desire more gifts** and **pray to the Father in Jesus' name** so we can take the **Body of Christ to another level**, and the world we see the **long-awaited manifestation** of the **children of God Amen.**

CHAPTER 22

THE HOLY SPIRIT GIVES THE POWER TO HEAL THE SICK

In the final words of our Lord and Saviour **Jesus Christ** in the **Gospel of Mark,** He gave the great commission and the signs that would follow believers.

"Go into all the world and preach the Gospel to all creation. These signs will accompany those who have believed in My name they will cast out demons, they will speak in new tongues; they will pick up serpents, and if they drink anything deadly, it will not hurt them; they will lay hands on the sick, and they will get well." **Mark, 16 15:17.**

I am going to zero-in on some keywords as the Holy Spirit leads. The first is they will **speak in new tongues** (praying in tongues is the source of POWER). There is **no Christianity without the Holy Spirit,** and a **Christian can't survive without the power of the Holy Spirit.**

I know how I feel when I first wake up and how I feel once I have prayed in the Spirit. The change that happens in my feeling is the **infusion of the power of the Holy Spirit.** It the same power that **Jesus said** is **greater than** the **power** that is in the **world.**

It is the same power from Acts 1:8. When the disciples had the infilling with this power, they were able to see the manifestation of what Jesus said in Mark 16, which were the signs that follow those who believe.

The **second word** the Holy Spirit wants to focus attention on is "**they will lay hands on the sick, and they will recover/get well.**" I believe religion often hinders the work of God, but God's timing is perfect. His **messengers** are **not recognized** by **their family** nor in **their country.**

I believe if a Christian can pray in the **Holy Ghost for multiple hours**, such people have the **power to heal** the sick according to the above verse in the **Gospel of Mark.**

According to the book Your Power in the Holy Spirit, John G Lake, one of the old school generals of God, is said to have **100,000 healings** recorded in **five years** of his ministry.

John G Lake also had an **experiment** conducted on him. **Bacteria** were placed on **his hands;** this activity was observed under a microscope, and to the amazement of those experimenting, the bacteria **died** when it came in contact with the **hands of John G Lake.**

The result from the experiment is the demonstration of the **Power of the Holy Spirit** on the **man of God.**

Another example of the power of God is with His **Prophet Elisha. A dead man's body** made **contact** with the **bones of Elisha** and **came alive**.

2 Kings 13:21: "And it happened that as a man was being buried [on an open bier], they saw a marauding band [coming]; and they **threw the man into Elisha's grave**. But when the [body of the] man [was being let down and] **touched the bones of Elisha**, he **revived and stood up on his feet.**"

It's time to let the power of the **Holy Spirit flow,** in an **orderly manner**, in the Church of Jesus Christ, and to **reduce all motivational sermons** and **preaching that build up the flesh.**

It's time for the true Church to **replicate** what the **early Church did,** and if your church can't do that, **then they are not the real deal.**

As **Apostle Paul** said in **Roman 1:16,** "For I am **not ashamed** of the Gospel (good news) *of Christ,* for it is God's power working unto salvation [for deliverance from eternal death] to everyone who believes *with* a personal trust *and* a confident surrender *and* firm reliance."

The Gospel is the **POWER working unto salvation. Salvation** comes from the **Greek word** *soteria,* which **means save, rescue, and deliver.**

Therefore, the Power of God can **save a soul, rescue us from any situation** and **deliver us from any health issue, including medical, and mental**.

We will **NEVER be ashamed** of the precious Gospel of Jesus Christ and the message of the **Cross.**

We will proclaim our **FAITH BOLDLY** because J**esus is Lord. Amen.**

It is only the **anointed message in a song that can change a life**, and the **lyrics MUST** mention the *source of the POWER.*

A song **without the anointing** is just another song listened to for a **short period,** but if a song is **anointed and if the name of Jesus, the blood of Jesus and/or the Holy Spirit are mentioned** in the lyrics to bring the anointing, then *the song will be listened to forever.*

Are you a Christian artist ashamed of the **only name** and **power** that can save a **person's soul?**

The Illuminati CANNOT save anybody's soul, and that is the Gospel truth.

If you call yourself a Christian artist, your **lyrics MUST incorporate** the name above all names, because there is power in the name of Jesus, and it's the power of the Holy Spirit that can **SAVE, RESCUE AND DELIVER**. Amen.

It's time for the Church to **WAKE UP**, and **stop selling out.**

Praise the Lord! I read that ***Demi Lovato*** got baptized, which means she has **repented** and has had a ***spiritual rebirth (she is born again)***. **Please** make sure you are **filled** with the **Holy Spirit**, as the **Holy Spirit is the only person who can help us along this journey. Welcome to the family** of the true living **God. Jesus is Lord. Amen.**

CHAPTER 23

THE HOLY SPIRIT HELPS US IN THE DISCERNMENT OF SPIRITS

In the book of **Hebrews**, the amplified version **Chapter 5:14** reads solid food is for the **[spiritually] mature**, whose senses are **trained** by practice to **distinguish** between what is **morally good** and *what is* **evil**.

The question that comes to mind is, how do we train our senses?

Galatians 4 verse 19b says **until Christ is [completely and permanently] formed within you.**

In other words, it's a **continuous process** of being in the Lord's presence, of **praying in the Holy Ghost**, of **praying the Word of God**, and of **r**eading/listening to the Word of God and **worship.**

Therefore, once we have a **regular** and **disciplined time** in **God's presence** doing all the **spiritual practices above**, it's fair to say we are training our **spiritual senses**; hence, we can **discern spirits** and **people around us.**

I know some people may **naturally** have the **gift of discernment of spirits,** but **I believe everybody can have it** if we spend **quality time** in the **Lord's presence** and are **sober-minded**. Don't forget, our enemies are **always watching us**, but what they don't know is that **we are watching them too, with spiritual eyes of discernment.**

Let's define the word *discernment*. According to Wikipedia, discernment is the **ability to obtain sharp perceptions** or to judge well.

In the above definition, let's zero-in on **sharp perception.**

At any point in time, a Christian **would know** if they are **sharp in the Spirit or not**. When a Christian is sharp, such a person has a *free flow with the Holy Spirit and is sensitive to the promptings of the Holy Spirit.*

In an article writing in www.happyhealthyandprosperous.com, it says:

"The Holy Spirit will frequently reveal things to us, warn us, or prompt us into prayer or action."

The Holy Spirit sees everything, He knows the **traps** and **snares** of our enemies. Our **closeness to the Holy Spirit** will enable us to **pick up the prompting and to NOT IGNORE THEM.**

An article in Christianity.com says, "**Discernment** has *historically been praised as a valuable trait, allowing those who possess it to avoid costly mistakes or misfortune.*"

Vocabulary.com says, "**Discernment** is **understanding something that's somewhat hidden or obscure.**"

Again, **nothing is hidden from the Holy Spirit**, so when He **prompts us to pray (by way of feeling a little heaviness on our heart, NEVER IGNORE IT),** it could be that our enemies are plotting some **evil plan.** This could happen **anywhere.**

One should **silently pray in the Spirit in one's heart**; *no one has to hear you.*

Another **critical point is**, for a Christian working in the secular world, as the saying goes, **YOU CANNOT TRUST ANYONE IN BABYLON.** The enemies of our **FAITH are plotting 24/7;** they have a hidden agenda for you. **So, be kind, walk in love**, but at the same time, be very **watchful.**

As for **public speakers, one must take authority over the vicinity** of where the speaking will take place, as there could be **demonic agents** among the people in your **audience**.

These **demonic agents** could release **various demons at you during your speaking.** You would **feel it** once they have done it, and the **Holy Spirit will tell you who it is.** *(Hopefully, you have the gift of discernment.)*

Another **painful experience a public speaker** faces is having an **energy VAMPIRE in the audience.** They will **suck one's energy, and you would feel the pain of them doing it,** and the only thing one could do is to endure the pain and man up. **Deal with the person in prayer when you get home.**

In the Bible, Potiphar's house was **blessed** because of **Joseph**, and Laban was **blessed** because of **Jacob**. The kingdom of darkness always knows when a **person is of the light and anointed by the true living God.**

Therefore, wherever the **child of God goes, they are after you**, from the gym to wherever.

Our enemies often need a **point of contact** to put an evil spirit on a Christian.

Below are various points of contact for an evil spirit to be deposited.

1. Music

2. Pictures

3. **A person**

4. **An object**

5. **Envelope**

6. **Premises**

7. **On a sermon message from YouTube**

8. **Food,/sweets**

9. **Phone calls**

I have experienced all the above.

Music

An evil spirit could be put in music, especially secular music, CDs or YouTube, and once a person listens to it, the evil spirit goes into a person.

Pictures

An evil spirit can be put on a picture, and when one is gazing at the beauty of the image, the evil demon is transferred.

A person

Evil people often use innocent people. I was in a university library years ago chatting with a cute girl; moments after the conversation, an evil spirit was attached to me. **It was a set-up.**

I have also gone to several **shops in a location I lived in the past**, and they used young ladies (to transfer the evil spirit) behind the till because they knew I **often chatted with them.**

It's not fair to use people to do their evil deeds because when I go to warfare prayer to ***remove the evil spirit***, the person they are using ***will get hurt.***

An object

An evil spirit could be attached to any object and given to you, so be careful; the Holy Spirit will always tell you.

I am not going to elaborate on the rest of the items I mentioned above, but anything that *involves our five senses CAN be used.*

When an evil spirit is transferred to a person, and you are **using an electronic device, such as a computer**, it can *mess up the computer, disrupt it and crash.*

Finally, please don't be **taking food or sweets from folks;** this I have also **experienced** as a way to transfer an *evil spirit.*

The purpose of the evil spirit could be to control, manipulate, monitor and put a spirit of fear on a person. It could also be to **initiate** a person into the kingdom of **darkness.**

So, don't be alarmed; *it is the way it is.*

I am going to **conclude** this with the first verse of the **hymn "Onward Christian Soldiers."**

Onward, Christian soldiers! *Marching as to war,*

with the *cross of Jesus* going on before.

Christ, the royal **master,** *leads his armies on:*

forward into battle till the fight is won!

Onward, Christian soldiers, marching as to war,

with the cross of Jesus going on before.

Remember *Jesus Christ* is the **Light** and **Saviour of the world.**

CHAPTER 24

THE HOLY SPIRIT'S GIFT OF FAITH

All gifts of the Holy Spirit are **essential**, and they have their place, but the **gift of faith** has a **special place** in our relationship with God.

If we have a relationship with a person we value, we would like it to be **cordial.**

Likewise, in our relationship with God, we want our relationship with our **Heavenly Father to be cordial.** This way, we can trust Him with things we don't yet understand.

God always wants us to trust Him no matter what.

Therefore, we need an **element of faith** to please **God.**

Before I proceed, let's **define** the word **faith**. I am going to use the Amplified classic edition:

Hebrews 11:1 Now faith is the assurance (the confirmation, [a]the title deed) of the things [we] hope for, being the proof of things [we] **do not see *and* the conviction of their reality [faith perceiving as real fact what is not revealed to the senses].**

Our senses are given to us for this physical world, and this includes our eyes, but let us not forget that we are dual creatures, i.e., we have our physical body, but we are also Spirit.

According to the revelation God gave the Apostle Paul, when we got saved, things changed. **Ephesians 2:6 in the Amplified Bible** (AMP) says,

6 And He raised us up together with Him [when we believed], and **seated us with Him** in the **heavenly *places*,** [because we are] in **Christ Jesus.**

Therefore, we know things are **not always revealed to our senses. A Christian has the upper hand,** as we see things in the spirit realm with our spiritual eyes. **Things are made known to us by our Spirit.**

Let me also point out that, **the more we are in the Spirit**, the more things will be **revealed to us.**

Our lifestyle pleases and honors God, and when we mess up, we **confess** our mistakes, and **He forgives us,** as **He sees us through His Son and the precious blood shed for our past, present, and future mess-ups.** (I was thinking the other day that God forgives instantly, but man often does not and even writes one off.) However, what **pleases God is our FAITH.**

The Importance of Faith in Our Relationship with God

The Bible says that without faith, it's impossible to please God. In the Amplified version (my favorite version of the Bible), it says, "But without faith it is impossible to [**walk with God** and] please Him, **for whoever comes [near] to God must [necessarily] believe that God exists** and that He rewards those who [earnestly and diligently] seek Him.

Let me zero-in on **WALK with God.** The verse says to walk with God, we need faith, and all Christians who believe in God have faith to a degree. The fact that we *walk and fellowship with what is not visible indicates it's supernatural.*

I guess that's why when we first got saved, we were all given a measure of faith because **without faith, one cannot believe in what they can't see.**

Romans 12.3, Amplified, says, "As **God has apportioned** to each a degree of faith [and a purpose-designed for service]."

According to the Amplified version, **one's faith is in accordance with one's calling** (purpose designed for service) and each person's service varies and differs from one believer to another.

Therefore, if our faith is in **accordance with our calling,** and if we all have different callings, then it means **we have different levels of faith;** therefore, churches need the **five-fold ministry** in which we have the **apostles and prophets, etc**. So the body can be **fully equipped**.

Apostle Paul says that **He prayed in tongues** more that you all, which means **God graced him to do that,** as his calling as an Apostle would **require** that he **operated at a high level of faith.**

In as much as some of us know the ways to **build up our faith**, its **grace** that **enables us to carry the duty out.** It's one thing to know and another thing to do it, and its **grace that helps us to be diligent in doing.**

Therefore, those who have and operate in the gift of faith please God. **The question is,** can we all have and **operate in the gift of faith**?

I believe so; however, **our reason for wanting** this **gift** has to be for the **work of the Lord.**

As I mentioned earlier, it takes **God to grace us with a diligent spirit** to do what needs to be done to operate in the **gift of faith continuously.**

THE HOLY SPIRIT'S GIFT OF FAITH, PART 2

The spirit of faith, according to *2 Corinthians 4:13,* is to believe and then speak. Our *Lord Jesus Christ* also calls this *great faith.*

Great is defined as the ability, quality, or eminence considerably above average. **Great faith** is mentioned by *Jesus twice in the scriptures,* but I am only going to **focus** on **Matthew 8: verse 8** when the centurion said, "**SAY the word,** and my *servant shall be healed."* The centurion went further to say that he also was a *person subject to authority.*

Talking about *authority,* Jesus said in *Matthew 28:18, "All authority (all power of absolute rule) in heaven and on earth* has been given to Us." Since we are Jesus' followers, we have the authority Jesus had, which is all power of absolute rule in Heaven and Earth.

People in authority know that when they give a *command,* it must be carried out. Therefore, when we *say/speak the Word of God, it must happen.*

Spiritual warfare, for instance, is **saying and speaking** the *Word of God,* and **it works**; it's the reason I am *still standing.*

God has given us the **tools** (*His Word, the Holy Spirit, the Name of Jesus, and the Blood of Jesus),* and these *tools are mighty in God*, but to top all this up, He has given us *authority.*

I was in *New York recently*, and I visited, the *Brooklyn Tabernacle*, the church I got *water baptized;* this was *around 20 years ago*.

In a meeting with **Pastor Lincoln** at *the Brooklyn Tabernacle*, I couldn't help but *reminisce* the time when I was a *baby Christian*, and I would go to him for advice, and how the *Christian walk seemed hard*.

I still *seek counsel from my pastor,* as *accountability is vital* for a Christian, but in regard to spiritual warfare, I have *learned* a lot *over the years*.

In my journey, I have seen how speaking the Word of God works. In my numerous encounters with spiritual warfare, I have seen *speaking/ saying the Word of God work over and over again*.

The *Holy Spirit* will also *show us* the **damage** caused *to the enemy* by *SAYING/SPEAKING the Word of God.*

The **good thing about prayer/***saying the Word of God* is, you can do it **alone** in the *four corners of your room*. Thank God for meetings with fellow believers and praying together, *as it has its place*.

However, when the enemy **wants to attack you,** he will make sure you are **alone**; hence, *one MUST know how to be alone and pray,* just like our **Saviour Jesus Christ.** He often *prayed alone.*

Over the years, *I have cultivated the habit of praying alone*, and as an *introvert*, it's my *preferred way to pray.*

Back to the **spirit of faith**, when one is in the *zone/in the spirit*, one is in the *atmosphere of POWER*, and in the place where our spoken words are *more effective.*

We also have to realize that *faith and power deplete; we have to keep on topping* them up; that's why the Bible says we should *pray without ceasing (1 Thessalonians 5:16).*

Another *critical aspect* of the spirit of faith can be found in *Jude 20*, "But you, beloved, build yourselves up [founded] on your *most holy Faith* [[a]make progress, rise like an edifice higher and higher], praying in the Holy Spirit."

The **above verse** does *two things: it builds up faith and power*. It's fair to say if one has *spiritual power, one has faith, and if one has faith, one has spiritual power.*

What we must also *bear in mind*, just like anything else in life, is *we get out of a thing what we put into it.*

The phrase "*according to*" (used by Jesus Christ in regard to faith and Apostle Paul about power) is *defined as in proportion or relation to.*

Let's start with the verse from *Jesus Christ, from Matthew 9:29* (Amplified): "According to your faith [your trust and confidence in My power and My ability to heal] it will be done to you."

We have to have *trust and confidence in the Word's power and ability.* In the beginning was the *Word, and the Word became flesh (Jesus).*

The Bible also says that faith comes by hearing the Word of God *(Romans 10:17)*.

In other words, it's by the *proportion of us hearing* the **Word of God** that will *equate to our faith*.

The other verse that used the word *according* was written by *Apostle Paul* and he used it concerning power, and this can be found in *Ephesians 3.20 (Amplified).*

"Now to Him who is able to [carry out His purpose and] do super-abundantly more than all that we dare *ask or think* [infinitely beyond our greatest prayers, hopes, or dreams], **according** to *His power that is at work* within us."

Looking at both of these two verses that have the word **according** indicates the ***onus is on us;*** we get out what we put in.

Even if we have the spirit of faith ***as a gift, we still have to work it.*** A proper and powerful technique is ***praying in our most holy faith (gets rid of doubt) for an hour or so and releasing it through the Spoken Word of God; now you will see the enemy on the run.***

An ***indication of faith is peace***, even if we haven't ***physically seen the manifestation.***

CHAPTER 25

THE HOLY SPIRIT'S GIFT OF DISCERNMENT

I received a text a couple of days ago, which included a number to reset my Facebook password, and the text took me on a walk down memory lane.

I left social media (Facebook and Twitter) 3 or 4 years ago. The reason was **MANIPULATION.**

This manipulation came from the **secular** and **religious worlds.**

These manipulators are pure evil folks, and how they sleep at night is beyond me, especially those who use scriptures to manipulate.

My relationship with the **Lord** has become **so much better.** It has also gotten **stronger** after leaving both of the above mentioned social media platforms.

At the minute, I am only on YouTube, and this is another device that manipulators use to target people; however, if their manipulation gets out of hand, I will undoubtedly delete my account and leave.

When I left Facebook and Twitter, I said, "Good riddance," mainly because of the **so many voices coming** at me, and these voices had their **hidden agendas.**

When a person gets into the habit of reducing outside voices, one can **hear God's voice clearer.**

The internet has many advantages because of its readily available information at one's disposal. Still, it also has its disadvantages, in that it enables folks to gain access to you, which wouldn't be the case without the internet. Some people's access is **detrimental** mainly due to manipulation (**you can't trust anyone in Babylon**).

They also use these social media platforms to **access one's consciousness**, which enables them to **transfer and steal one's virtues and spiritual gifts and to take one's energy.**

If anybody wants to **converse with me**, do it **directly by sending me an email, etc.**, as I will **ignore entirely indirect messages**. It's fair to say I have learned most manipulative **tricks, and they suck.**

So, let me **reiterate:** if anybody has anything to say, do it directly by sending an email **(come off your high horse). I WILL NOT entertain any silly** YouTube indirect messages or your **use of magic to get me to respond.**

If you **want prayers (and wish me to add you to my prayer list)**, send me an **email directly (again come off your high horse); I will not respond to any indirect request.**

All the above leads me to the next spiritual gift, which is the gift of discernment.

The **gift of discernment** is one of the **essential gifts** any human can **desire** (you have to be **born again** though).

My **definition of discernment** is a **supernatural ability** to know about a **person** or **situation** without the **necessary information** revealed to **one's senses.**

If a person is **Holy Spirit-filled** and **regularly prays in the Holy Ghost**, then it is i**nevitable that information will be divulged to that** *person*. Many people can pray in the Holy Spirit, but they *don't do it regularly*. I think this is a *huge mistake.*

When praying in our prayer language, *we are destroying the plans and works of our enemies*, and that's *why our enemies' evil plots are not working*. They might think their schemes are working, *but the Word of the only true Living God* said, "*No weapon formed on us shall prosper.*" Hence, *I choose to believe and trust the Word of the Lord.*

The Bible says in *1 Corinthians 14:2 (Amplified):*

"For one who speaks in an [unknown] tongue speaks not to men but to God, for no one understands or catches his meaning, because in the [Holy] Spirit he utters secret truths and hidden things [not obvious to the understanding]."

Therefore, by praying in the Holy Ghost, not only are we *possessing the mind of God, but the gift of discernment is built up and getting stronger and sharper.*

As we pray in this way (in tongues), *hidden truths and hidden things not apparent to our understanding* are being revealed to us. In other words, things that are *concealed by our enemies are made known to us*.

Another way to look at it is playing the *game of chess with our enemies*, and the *Holy Ghost is supernaturally helping us to make the right moves. Consequently, we are putting the manipulators and our enemies into CHECK-MATE.*

I come across a lot of people, and as an observer of humanity and human nature, I have to say *THE HOLY SPIRIT is the REAL DEAL. The Holy Spirit is the INCOMPARABLE POWER of a CHRISTIAN.*

Most people are empty on the inside, live in fear and are secretly crying out for a better way (the better way is the Gospel of Jesus Christ). They might have the money, but they have no PEACE.

When *ministers manipulate fellow Christians by using the Word of God, they are merely dishonoring our Lord Jesus Christ*, as *Jesus didn't need to do that.*

When *Jesus* appeared to His disciples after His resurrection in *John 21:15,* the *Bible says after they had finished eating*, Jesus said to *Simon Peter, do you love? He said this three times,* indicating Peter's level of assignment.

The point I want to *draw out here is that when people want to manipulate someone, they usually do it when there is a strain on one's physical condition,* such as an *empty stomach/being hungry. But not Jesus,* because *He knows we have free will;* therefore, He made sure Peter was in the *right frame of mind. After they had finished eating, the Bible says, Jesus popped up the question.*

God gives individual spiritual gifts to specific people for a reason, NOT to be stolen or transferred to another person. To those who have gifts from God, you have to take *FULL OWNERSHIP of what our Heavenly Father has bestowed on us.*

So, when we are *late to discern and find ourselves in a pickle, as we often do, we must call upon the Lord. He is good to be faithful.*

In Psalm 120. 1-4:

In my *distress,* I *cried* to the *Lord*, and He *answered me.*

2 *Deliver me*, O Lord, from *lying lips and from deceitful tongues.*

3 What shall be given to you? Or what more shall be done to you, you deceitful tongue?—

4 Sharp arrows of a [mighty] warrior, with [glowing] coals of the broom tree!

The Lord *often gives us instructions,* but as *typical human*s, we like to *listen more to someone (a human) whom we can see and idolize.*

For the most part, ***people don't knowingly disobey God***, but it comes with the journey of life; one gets tricked.

People want to listen to sermons (which is good); however, the message of the sermon or the preacher's message ***could be different from the specific instructions the Holy Spirit gave you for a particular situation.***

I am ***not pointing any fingers***. However, ***in the name of the Lord, please don't use the Word of the Lord to manipulate people for self-purpose*** or ***any other purpose.***

Being a Christian is excellent, ***but*** because man is involved, ***one has to learn the tricks, games, and manipulation of the Church.***

Yes, ***the manipulation will hurt for a while***, but ***God will heal the pain***, and one ***MUST*** continue in the ***faith.***

I have spoken to ***several people who got hurt in the Church*** and went to the ***dark side,*** which is going from o***ut of the frying pan and into the fire.***

From ***experience, we become wiser*** and are ***aware of the tricks and traps of unpleasant people whom life brings our way to grow us.***

Please never for a second blame God for the shortcomings of man (in and out of Church). Their negative actions can make us ***stronger, smarter, and better people if we allow them to.***

To those who have ***left the Church*** due to one reason or another, ***ask the Lord to re-connect you to a church of His choice.***

Learn from the ***pain of the past,*** and go with a ***discerning spirit.***

CHAPTER 26

THE HOLY SPIRIT'S GIFT OF MIRACLES

The word *miracle* is defined in the Cambridge Dictionary as "an _unusual_ and _mysterious_ _event_ that is thought to have been caused by **God** because it does not _follow the natural laws of nature_."

I want to point out that **God is above** all natural laws and laws of nature.

Another definition of *miracle*: "*an extraordinary* and welcome event that is *not explicable by natural or scientific laws* and is therefore attributed to a *divine agency*."

To *receive a miracle* or to *perform a miracle*, one **MUST believe** and be *expectant*.

Kathryn Kuhlman has a book titled *I believe in Miracles,* and guest what? *God used her to perform many miracles of healing.*

According to Wikipedia, the *gift of miracles* is *imparted to individuals by the power of the Holy Spirit.*

This gift, like all other gifts of the **Holy Spirit**, is **supernatural. The Holy Spirit in every Christian is supernatural**, and it's the **same power that was used to perform miracles** in the **Old and New Testaments** and to **raise Jesus from the dead.**

Examples of this **power at work: David killing Goliath, Samson killing a lion with his bare hands, Moses** parting the **Red Sea,** and the list goes on. In the **New Testament**, we see **Jesus turning water into wine, raising dead – Lazarus, etc.).**

Belief is the **cornerstone** for **performing** and **receiving** a **miracle.** To believe for the **miraculous**, one has to be **deep in the spirit/zone.** In other words, one **MUST detach oneself from the natural** and have **one's mind and consciousness set on heavenly things.**

To walk in the **dimension of miracles**, one has to be **focused more in the spirit realm than in the physical realm.** When one is in such an **atmosphere,** things of this world become so **small, immaterial and irrelevant.**

A person deep in the spirit/heavenly zones would see **themselves bigger and higher than the affairs of this world** ("Greater is He that is in you than he that is in the world," **1 John 4:4**).

What we **call** a **miracle in the natural world** is referred to as **normal in the spirit world,** and since a Christian – saved and born-again – **operates in two realms (the spiritual and the natural),** they have the **potential and ability to perform miracles.**

A **mature Christian,** according to **Hebrews 6:4-5,** is

4 **enlightened**, who have **consciously tasted the heavenly Gift** and have become **sharers of the Holy Spirit,**

5 And have **felt how good the Word of God is** and the **mighty powers of the age and world to come.**

However, the above verse must be *maintained* and *used* because if *one doesn't use it, one will lose it.*

To consistently flow and *operate at a high level in the spirit* (performing miracles, etc.), the spirit realm *MUST be one's center of attention.*

Also, when *God* is *ready to use a person in the area of miracles*, He will make sure *such a person's heart's desire has been granted*, such as *a spouse*, as *one can't afford to be distracted.*

A person who would be used in this area is *someone who understands the POWER of the spoken words* and the *effect of idle words.* It is words *spoken that cause a miracle to happen* and *changes the dynamics in the spirit world*, and the *spirit world controls our natural world.* Everything is connected.

Another *critical point*, as seen in the Bible, is *when the Lord is with a person*, such a person will be *flowing in POWER and FAITH* (for God to be with us, we must be with Him). *Draw near to God and He will draw near to you (James 4:8).*

The Bible says in *1 Samuel 3:19,* "Now *Samuel grew,* and the *Lord was with him*, and *He let none of his words [a]fail [to be fulfilled]*." Another version says, "*None* of *Prophet Samuel's words fell to the ground.*"

When a person's spirit and mind are trained, then *one's thoughts and words can affect and change any atmosphere.*

People accept whatever the natural world throws at them, such as *medical conditions*, but as a *Christian*, if something *doesn't line up with the word of God, we reject it and start to speak the word of God over it.*

The more one is in the ***natural, the less one is in the spirit, and the less power to believe and perform miracles. Smith Wigglesworth didn't read the newspaper.*** He didn't allow his ***visitors bring to newspapers into his house, and I am sure he didn't watch television either***, and that's why he could ***perform all the miracles he did.*** He ***totally walked with God, consumed by the Holy Spirit's presence***.

We become what we feed our flesh with; to be effective, ***spiritual, and powerful,*** we must ***continuously set our mind on things above.*** We must ***starve the flesh and feed the spirit.***

In other words, we have to be in the ***spirit/zone for the POWER to flow.***

How come the ***Body of Christ doesn't have many Smith Wigglesworths and Kathryn Kuhlmans?*** I believe there is a ***correlation between the time one spends in God's presence and the miracles God can perform through such an individual.***

There are ***different ways of getting God's power (the anointing) on us.*** Our ***responsibility is finding what approach works for us.*** For example, ***Smith Wigglesworth and Kathryn Kuhlman*** had **different prayer styles and different methods of spending time in God's presence.** ***The basis is the same – prayer and the word, etc. – but the techniques are different.***

That's why the ***shepherd boy David*** couldn't flow in ***King Saul's armor.*** Not only had he ***not tested it***, as his ***method and relationship with God was different.***

We must find ***our unique flow with God*** because the ***world is hungry for the truth, and it is waiting for the Children of God.***

When people don't know the truth (Word of God), they accept anything the world and life (doctors) throw at them. A skilled Christian,

on the other hand, wouldn't receive such **reports and situations that don't line up with the truth (Word of God).**

When people **can't receive the truth of the Gospel, they suffer and believe the wrong report, and they remain totally clueless about the power of the Gospel.** The reason why I am proud of my Christian faith and of the powerful Gospel of Jesus Christ is because I have **experienced it (the power of the Good news) over and over again.**

Now, **I wouldn't lie and say it's a comfortable or easy journey.** It's not. **There is a high price to pay**, but we are not alone; **Jesus is with us all the way. Ultimately, it's worth it, as one is being a blessing to mankind.**

CHAPTER 27

THE HOLY SPIRIT HELPS US OBEY THE VOICE OF GOD

As a *messenger of God*, it's easy to hear the *Lord's voice* and to *brush it away*; however, it's certainly *not a wise thing to do*.

The Lord is *always ready to speak through us*, but we *MUST be available*. Recently, the Lord has been revealing to me certain *energy VAMPIRES*. All of them call themselves *Christians*, and my take is, if you are a Christian, *why can't you connect with God so He can fill up your cup*?

Social media, such as YouTube, is one of the *devices they use*. These vampires *post sermons, their music, or even their interviews online*. When one listens to whatever they post, *they can connect to one's soul/ spirit, and at night or early hours of the morning, when one is asleep, these energy vampires come and suck a person's energy*. It is *painful* and *uncomfortable* for the person they are stealing energy from, *but what do they care, right?*

Energy vampires also *come to churches for the sole purpose of stealing people's energy during worship*. I received *confirmation* of this when I noticed a *young lady* come in and *sit behind me*. During the greeting time, *I had a small chat* with her *before the worship started.*

The worship was excellent, and ***I connected to the Spirit of God, and was flowing in the Spirit.*** I then felt ***excruciating pain on my thigh (lap)***; I knew what was happening. ***I wanted to know who was doing it. Immediately after worship before we took our seats, this young lady (sitting behind me) left and never returned.*** The ***Holy Spirit said it was her.***

Energy vampires coming to churches ***to steal energy*** is a ***common practice,*** as this has happened ***many times before in different churches.*** I have had a ***pastor in a particular church do the same;*** it's wrong.

If you call yourself a ***Christian and go around stealing people's energy***, I consider you a ***FAKE Christian***, for if you were a REAL Christian, you would be able to ***connect with God via the Holy Spirit. I am not going to mention names (as is my custom), but you need to stop because I know who all of you are (some famous names).*** Now I do my best not to listen to your music or interviews as I know you ***target the folks you want to steal from in your opportune time.***

I tried to ignore this, by not writing about it and doing the best to protect myself, but as I read the Bible, the passage that the Lord used to speak to me was ***Ezekiel 33: 7-9 Amplified***, let's read:

"Now as for you, son of man, ***I have made you a watchman*** for the house of Israel; ***so you shall hear a message from My mouth and give them a warning from Me.*** 8 When I say to the wicked, ***'O wicked man, you will certainly die,'*** and ***you do not speak to warn the wicked from his way, that wicked man will die because of his sin***; but ***I will require his blood from your hand.*** 9 But if you on your part ***warn the wicked man to turn from his [evil] way and he does not turn from his [evil] way, he will die in his sin***; but you have ***saved your life.***"

I know the kingdom of ***darkness is very persistent***, but the ***truth is you could hurt yourself.*** Well, I have ***WARNED you and obeyed God.***

One gets to a particular stage in the Christian walk and life when one has ***seen a lot and observed life and people inside out***. I must confess such experience is an ***intangible asset as wisdom comes from past occurrences***.

One then realizes what matters most, which is to walk out ***one's salvation with fear and trembling***. One only warns when the ***Lord asks one to do so***.

I don't care about what others are doing. ***I observe and mind my business and protect myself from energy vampires who like to come at night.***

Apostle Paul fought to the end, and that's what ***we have to do***, especially when we have a different ***Jesus highly promoted in Christianity today.***

Apostle Paul also ***warned us about this time*** in ***Galatians 1:8:*** "But even if an angel from heaven or we should preach to you a ***gospel contrary to and different from that which we preached to you***, let him be accursed (anathema, devoted to destruction, ***doomed to eternal punishmen***t)!"

So please don't be deceived; stay close to the Holy Spirit. If there ever was a time to have and to ***use the gift of praying in tongues continuously***, it's ***NOW, as deception has gotten out of control.***

As in Roman 8: 26- 28, we are praying God's perfect will. Let's read:

So too the ***[Holy] Spirit*** comes to our aid *and* bears us up in our weakness; for we do not know what prayer to offer *nor* how to offer it worthily as we ought, but the Spirit Himself goes to meet our supplication *and* pleads in our behalf with ***unspeakable yearnings and groanings too deep for utterance.***

27 And He Who searches the hearts of men knows what is in the mind of the [Holy] Spirit [what His intent is], because the Spirit intercedes *and* pleads [before God] on behalf of the saints according to *and* in **harmony with God's will.**

28 We are assured *and* know that [God being a partner in their labor] **all things work together and are [fitting into a plan] for good to and for those who love God and are called according to [His] design and purpose.**

Don't **worry about God's plan for your life.** As you pray in the Holy Ghost, **God's plan is unfolding. Amen.**

To the lost, we are praying for you. It's time to **give up the dark** and **come to the LIGHT. Jesus Christ** is and will always be the **light** and **Savior** of the **world.**

You have been **deceived long enough**, it's **time to embrace the truth. There is ONLY one truth, and it is JESUS CHRIST, the Son of the Living God.**

I am sure there are a **lot of Ruths out there**, am praying God will open your eyes. For some, they have been in darkness for **generations,** but the **God** whom I **serve** is **able and will deliver you. Amen.**

Enemies **try to trap people**, but when one is a **Holy Ghost praying individual, their plans fail.**

Agents of the kingdom of darkness, please don't let them **use you to carry out evil deeds. It is very dangerous; you can't come against a child of God and succeed. You are not coming against me but God.** Don't let them use you.

Finally, brethren, Remember the Word of the Lord. He will **never leave us nor forsake us** because **He loves us. AMEN**. No matter **how challenging this Christian walk gets, remember Jesus loves you.**

CHAPTER 28

THE HOLY SPIRIT CAN LEAD US DAILY

It's good to have a plan and a strict routine, but it's even better when we allow the ***Holy Spirit to lead us daily.*** The reason I used the word *daily* is that the ***Holy Spirit is a gentleman,*** and He will ***never force us*** to do anything. Not only that, sometimes, when ***God sends us to a place,*** we ***seldom know what it's for or how long we will be there.***

We should always get into the habit of saying, "***Holy Spirit, what we are we doing today? What's next?***"

Let's not forget He ***(the Holy Spirit) knows everything.*** The Bible says in ***James 2:4b,*** "You do not have because you do not ask [it of God]."

Another vital verse to ***confess daily*** is *Jeremiah 33:3,* "***Call to Me, and I will answer you, and tell you [and even show you] great and mighty things, [things which have been confined and hidden], which you do not know and understand and cannot distinguish*** (Amplified)."

When our minds are in the habit of ***focusing on God,*** not only will God give us ***perfect peace,*** but He will ***drop revelations and show us the plots and plans of our enemies in our spirit.***

The Holy Spirit knows the tricksters, manipulators, liars, and cheats.

The ***Holy Spirit*** knows the ***hearts of men and all the hidden agendas*** of the people trying to pull us towards them.

Jesus (the most excellent empath ever) knew the heart of man, and so can we. ***Mark 2:8*** (and all over the Gospels) reads, "Immediately Jesus, being fully aware [of their hostility] *and* knowing in His spirit that they were thinking this, said to them, 'Why are you debating *and* arguing about these things in your hearts?'"

In the last section, I mentioned an energy vampire who messed with me during worship at a particular church; the ***Holy Spirit has revealed that it was all planned, and she was part of a plot.***

The ***Holy Spirit*** had to bring to my remembrance other churches that have done the same thing in the past.

They ***suck one's POWER*** so they can ***manipulate a person.*** When a ***person is powerless, such a person is vulnerable. POWERLESS EQUALS VULNERABILITY.***

These activities are wrong, especially in a church that has Jesus Christ as its Head. Such practices are witchcraft, plain, and simple; it's all part of the doctrine of the devil.

When the body of Christ engages in these acts, it makes the Lord hide His face from them. ***Ezekiel 39:24*** (Amplified) reads, ***"I dealt with them in accordance with their uncleanness and their transgressions, and I hid My face from them."***

When the ***Lord hides His Face***, then His presence will not be in such ***particular vicinity.***

You must choose: do you want God's Presence or not? If you continue practicing doctrines of the devil, ***I guarantee God's presence WILL NEVER BE AMONG YOU.*** Your services will be mechanical and dry, and no lives will be changed or touched by the ***POWER OF GOD.***

Every action causes a reaction, so we have to be careful of our actions. People's actions enable pictures to be painted, and a picture is ***worth a thousand words***.

Nothing can be said that hasn't been said before, but I guess somethings just don't change, right?

Jesus Christ owns the Church, as He said to Peter in ***Matthew 16:18,*** "I say also unto thee, That thou art Peter, and upon this rock, I will build My Church; ***and the gates of hell shall not prevail against it.***"

As we can see, Jesus said, "I will build ***MY Church***," so any practice done in a church that ***can't be found in the Bible is wrong*** and we should be ready to ***FLEE that church.***

So, please HEAR the Word of the Lord and amend your ways.

The Word of the Lord says in ***James 5:19,*** "My brothers and sisters, if anyone among you strays from the truth *and* falls into error and [another] one turns him back [to God], 20 let the [latter] one know that the one who has turned a sinner from the error of his way will save that ***one's soul from death and cover a multitude of sins*** [that is, obtain the pardon of the many sins committed by the one who has been restored]."

We certainly live in exciting times, ***so let's have our eyes on the RIGHT price.*** It's not about creating a ***name for ourselves, or our vision;*** it is merely about doing the ***will of the Father.***

Apostle Peter rightly says in 1 Peter 1:24 -25:

"All flesh is like grass,

And all its glory like the flower of grass.

The grass withers

And the flower falls off,

But the word of the Lord endures forever."

And this is the word [the good news of salvation] which was preached to you.

CHAPTER 29

THE HOLY SPIRIT SHOWS US THE SYNAGOGUES OF SATAN

There was a time when I looked forward to **Sunday mornings** because it was **Church day.** Here is a little bit of history about the Sabbath. The Sabbath should be Saturday. Sunday as a day of worship is **pagan (sun-day – the day they worship the SUN), but that's a topic for another book.**

There was also a time that I never **MISSED going to church on a Sundays**, but with **great regret**, I have to say it's not so anymore.

Trust me, it's a good thing to go to the **House of the Lord** with **fellow believers and to fellowship**, and **I miss the good old days.** The question you probably have on your mind is, **what changed?**

What changed is a combination of things. I have **grown and awoken spiritually,** and I have **seen a lot.**

An **important point I want to emphasize is, even if I don't go or haven't found a place of worship** doesn't mean that the **quality time I spend in the Lord's presence** has **changed or decreased.** By the grace of God, **I can confidently say I have an excellent relationship with God,**

my Saviour Jesus Christ, and the Holy Spirit. To God be the glory, as this is all by **God's grace.**

Going back to what I mentioned earlier about looking forward to Sundays, and never missing church on a Sunday, I would like to say as my **eyes opened, and with all the spiritual attacks and manipulation in the so-called House of God,** I knew I had to *take precautionary measures.*

Many years ago, when I started to see some **strange things occur in church**, I remember saying, "*This can't be God,* and *this is not of God. What is going on?"*

It was much later that I got to know that a **lot of churches had SOLD OUT; in other words, many of the churches and their leaders are part of secret societies,** and these secret societies *worship the god of this world. The god of this world is Lucifer.*

Consequently, some churches are controlled, and the *doctrine of demons has entered some churches.*

Now, we live in a *free world and society,* and if people *choose to worship the devil, fine. To each his own. I don't want that*, and I must say some churches that are part of this *abominable act have it as their aim is to get others involved and on their side.*

I have to work out my salvation as **Apostle Paul** wrote in the **Book of Philippians**. Let's read: "So then, my dear ones, just as you have always obeyed [my instructions with enthusiasm], not only in my presence, but now much more in my absence, continue to work out your salvation [that is, cultivate it, bring it to full effect, *actively pursue spiritual maturity*] with *awe-inspired fear and trembling [using serious caution and critical self-evaluation to avoid anything that might offend God or discredit the name of Christ]." Philippians 2:12 Amplified.*

In the above verse, it says we should *actively pursue spiritual maturity*; I one-hundred percentage believe I am an **OLD SOUL**.

There are certain things (as a result of being an **OLD SOUL**) *I can't do*, *such as bowing down to the devil or a false god. I ONLY BOW DOWN TO the true GOD AND MY SAVIOUR JESUS CHRIST, period.*

The above verse also says using *severe caution and critical self-evaluation to avoid anything that might offend God or discredit the name of Christ.* Again, I know the **OLD SOUL** in me knows that these warnings are very crucial. *I have an inner knowing and words won't do me justice if I try to explain.*

Therefore, this **OLD SOUL** *cares less about the lion's den or the fiery furnace.* Come to think of it, it's this *inner knowing and the firm conviction that our heroes of the Bible demonstrated* that we all look forward to seeing them when we get home to *Heaven.*

Unfortunately, many people in the so-called Church *are not Heaven-bound because they have bowed down in exchange for fortune and fame.*

Let's look at **King David** who we can attribute many of the writings of the psalms. *King David wasn't perfect; he loved cute, pretty women,* which was one of his weak points, but *NO ONE CAN QUESTION HIS LOVE FOR GOD.*

The Prophet Samuel said, "The Lord has sought out for Himself a man (David) after *His own heart*, and the Lord has appointed him as leader *and* ruler over His people" *1 Samuel 13:14.*

Also in the *Book of the Acts of Apostles*, Apostle Paul said He *(God)* raised David to be their king: of him He testified and said, *"I have found David* the son of Jesse, *a man after My own heart [conforming to My will and purposes], who will do all My will."*

God is looking for those who will do ***HIS WILL and HIS PUR-POSE,*** especially those who proclaim they are ***ministers of the Gospel.***

Does anyone ***think King David*** and the many other ***heroes in the Bible would bow down to the devil? Of course NOT.*** They ***would rather die. Judas bowed down and sold out our Saviour***, but what was the end for Judas?

The exciting thing about the Word of God is that it's timeless. All the ***mess going on in churches today*** is what the Lord has already spoken of in the ***Book of Revelation***.

In Revelation 2: 9 (Amplified):

'I know your suffering and your poverty (but you are rich), and how you are blasphemed *and* slandered by those who say they are Jews and are not, but are a ***synagogue of Satan [they are Jews only by blood, and do not believe and truly honor the God whom they claim to worship].***

Our Lord calls most of ***churches today "synagogues of Satan." If ministers and churches are part of ANY SECRET SOCIETY, then they certainly fit our Lord's description.***

PLEASE HEAR THE WORD OF THE LORD AND REPENT NOW. TOMORROW MIGHT BE TOO LATE.

Finally, when minsters and people bow down to false gods, then God can't shine through them. We know people in the Bible, such as ***Prophet Daniel and the three Hebrews boys,*** would rather die than bow down to a false god. ***Their faithfulness to God is honoured by the Lord.***

As we see in ***Daniel 2:46*** (NKJ): "Then ***King Nebuchadnezzar fell on his face, prostrate before Daniel***, and commanded that they should present an offering and incense to him."

When we allow God to shine, the WORLD WILL BOW DOWN TO THE ONE TRUE LIVING GOD. AMEN.

<h1 style="text-align:center">CHAPTER 30</h1>

THE HOLY SPIRIT HELPS TO EXPOSE THE KINGDOM OF DARKNESS

It has and always will be the intention of God that followers of **Jesus Christ** grow and be **conformed** to His **image.**

Romans 8:29: "For those whom He foreknew [of whom He was [a]aware and [b]loved beforehand], He also destined from the beginning [foreordaining them] to be **molded into the image of His Son** [and share inwardly His likeness], that He might become the firstborn among many brethren."

Our **spiritual journey** is for us to **grow from faith to faith and from glory to glory.**

Another version of the Bible puts it this way **(The Voice Version)** in Romans 8:29-30:

*From the **distant past**, His eternal love reached into the future.* You see, He knew those who would be His one day, and He chose them beforehand to be conformed to the image of His Son so that Jesus would be the firstborn of a new family of believers, all brothers, and sisters. **As for those He chose beforehand, He called them to a *different destiny* so**

that they would experience what it means to be made right with God and share in His glory.

In other words, ***Jesus Christ (God in the flesh)*** must be **formed in us.**

Apostle Paul put it this way:

Galatians 4:19: "My little children, for whom I am again suffering birth pangs until Christ is ***completely and permanently*** formed (molded) within you." ***Christ means the anointed one***.

The anointed one **MUST** be formed in us or ***people will die like mere men*** (Psalms 82:6).

The kingdom of darkness has its agenda, and it is hindering the children of God from ***growing into the image of God***.

These enemies of God are all over the place, from the ***church to the workplace to the fitness club, etc.***

As we approach this New Year, ***you will be exposed***; you will all ***be named and shamed for various witchcraft, demonic, and evil practices. Enough is enough.***

All the ways you ***manipulate and steal virtues*** and ***blessings from God's people*** will be ***exposed for the world to see***, for our Father's ***Kingdom*** suffers violence, and ***violence takes by force***.

In the words of Jesus, let's read Matthew 11: 12-13 (The Voice):

All of the prophets of old, all of the law—that was all prophecy leading up to the coming of John. *Now, that sort of prepares us for this very point, right here and now.* ***When John the Baptist[a] came, the kingdom of heaven began to break in upon us, and those in power are trying to clamp down on it—why do you think John is in jail?***

To the powers that be, we *can't allow* you to *hinder us. We WILL NOT BOW TO YOU,* and *we will not participate in any form of abominable lifestyle.*

We focus and aim to see *Christ (God) formed in us and to see the manifestation of the sons of God.*

Romans 8:19(Amplified): "For [even the whole] creation (all nature) waits expectantly *and* longs earnestly for God's sons to be made known *[waits for the revealing, the disclosing of their sonship]."*

For there is a *remnant* who would r*ather lay down their life* than *bow down or comprise.*

*FELLOW CHRISTIANS/REMNANT*S, IT'S TIME TO *STEP UP.* It's *also time to get rid of the mess and deception* that takes place in the *Church.*

Churches, YOU WILL *EXPOSED,* SO YOU *BETTER CHANGE YOUR WAYS.*

There is *nothing new under the sun.* The same hindrance – *not allowing your congregation to find the Kingdom of God* – happened in *Jesus' time*

Let's look at Matthew 23:13 (Amplified): "But woe to you, scribes and Pharisees, pretenders (hypocrites)! *For you shut the kingdom of heaven in men's faces; for you neither enter yourselves, nor do you allow those who are about to go in to do so."*

The Voice version of the Bible puts it this way: "Woe to you, you teachers of the law and Pharisees. *There is such a gulf between what you say and what you do. You will stand before a crowd and lock the door of the kingdom of heaven right in front of everyone; you won't enter the Kingdom yourselves, and you prevent others from doing so."*

Finally, let's meditate on Psalm 82 (the Voice Version) so we can have a vision for ***growth for sons of God and for justice in 2020.***

<u>**Psalm 82**</u> **provides an image of a heavenly scene in which God accuses His heavenly messengers of not caring for the poor and pursuing justice.**

1   The True God stands *to preside* over the *heavenly* council.

    He pronounces judgment on the so-called gods.

2   *He asks:* "**How long will you judge dishonestly**

    and be **partial to the wicked?**"

3   "**Stand up for the poor and the orphan;**

    advocate for the rights of the afflicted and those in need.

4   ***Deliver the poor and the needy**;*

    rescue them from their evil oppressors."

5   *These bullies are ignorant; they have no understanding of My ways.*

    So as they walk in darkness,

    the foundations of the earth tremble.

6   I said, ***"Though you are gods***[b]

    and children of the Most High,

7   ***You will die no differently than any mortal**;*

    you will fall like one of the princes."

8   Rise up, ***O True God**; **judge the rulers of the earth,***

    for all the ***nations*** are Yours.

CHAPTER 31

THE HOLY SPIRIT HELPS US WALK WITH GOD

Some people have been ordained before the foundation of the world to walk with God. In as much as we all have a free will, and sometimes as **dual beings (part divine and part flesh),** the flesh kicks in and wants its gratifications, but deep down, we know that those days are long gone and can never be returned.

God calls people at different times, and He stages one's life to walk with Him; for the most part, He allows us to taste the world, so the memory of the **lack of satisfaction and emptiness makes us never want to go back to the world.**

It is a remarkable thing **to walk with God** and to be an **empath,** as one can easily **read the energy** of any vicinity and the energy on people without the people around saying a word. One knows the plots of which people (enemies) are planning. **Nothing needs to be said (no confrontation);** one should **distance** oneself from such person/people.

Genesis 5:24 (Amplified): "And [in reverent fear and obedience] **Enoch walked with God**; and he was not [found among men], because God took him [away to be home with Him]."

In other words, **Enoch had a close and intimate relationship with God, and one day, Enoch vanished.** I have also read or heard somewhere that Enoch knew too much. You see, when one is close to God's divine nature, He **(God) shares secrets with His children.**

The **Bible also says that Noah walked with God**. Hence, Noah knew beforehand about the flood and he prepared.

In some instances, a **person who walks with God knows never to do certain things.** They may not know **how to articulate why**, but they know particular action(s) are one-hundred percent NO NOs.

David divinely puts it this way in the **first Psalm:**

Blessed (happy, fortunate, prosperous, and enviable) is the man who walks *and* lives not in the counsel of the ungodly [following their advice, their plans and purposes], nor stands [submissive and inactive] in the path where sinners walk, nor sits down [to relax and rest] where the scornful [and the mockers] gather.

2 But his delight *and* desire are in the law of the Lord, and on His law (the precepts, the instructions, the teachings of God) he habitually meditates (ponders and studies) by day and by night.

The grace to do the above in Psalm 1 comes **directly from the Holy Spirit; it's the same Holy Spirit that helps us to not miss the mark.** It's not automatic; **one has to open one's mouth and pray in the Holy Spirit as it's the power from this exercise that keeps** us from falling short as a Christian of God's commandments.

There is something about **loving God** that the world will never be able to **fathom**; it is also **tough to comprehend.**

When one walks with the Lord, one has to **find what is close to God's heart** that *needs fixing or being looked after,* and as God told His son David in **Psalm 2:8, "Ask of me, and I will give you."**

There are a **lot of issues in our society that need God's miraculous touch**, as God's representation of Earth, we need to find a cause to support, and **God will grace us to carry it out.**

So let's find a cause for the betterment of mankind, and place **God's hand** on it as we begin **2020.**

It's interesting how people often say, **"So-and-so is going to happen this year,"** and they have their **so-called prophecies.** I have nothing against prophecies. **Unfortunately,** I have heard a lot of **false ones over the years,** so I like to stand clear of people with their so-called words from the Lord.

As our **dual individuality** of **part God (the Holy Spirit lives in us)** and **part man,** we should make it a **habit to hear God,** who lives in us.

Obviously, to hear from God, one has to love His presence (for the most part). To love God's presence, one has to love God. In fact, God is always with us, but we are **not always aware of his presence.**

We have to **keep the faith,** to keep on **pressing on,** and the Lord will give us the desires of our heart. As the Lord said in **Zechariah 8:9, "Thus says the Lord of hosts: Let your hands be strong *and* hardened."** There is **NO TIME FOR A FAITH BREAK, FOR THE JUST MUST ALWAYS LIVE BY FAITH.**

Our Faith grows and we become stronger as we regularly love being in the presence of the Holy Spirit

Sensing the Lord/**Holy Spirit** will often put a smile on one's face. It is such a **sweet presence**, and an unexplainable peace. As the Bible puts it, the Peace that passes all understanding.

As humans, we all want and **pray for peace.**

However, for a country to go into **three-day mourning because one of its top prominent citizens was assassinated** indicates that we **have not started 2020 on the right track, in my opinion.**

The atmosphere for safety and peace has just shifted. **President Trump** did what he said **President Obama** might do in **2011. The Word of the Lord says in Psalm 2.10, "Therefore, you kings, be wise; be warned you rulers of the Earth."**

As a result of the **assassination of an Iranian general, Americans** around the world have t**o start watching their backs.** This is certainly not the best way to live.

We reap what we sow, as God cannot be mocked.

An important spiritual law which most people are ignorant about is, what we allow in our heart.

The Bible says, "Out of the abundance of the heart the mouth speaks **(Matthew 12:34)."** It can also be said that out of the **abundance of our heart is what is manifested in one's life.**

Therefore, **we must be watchful**, so the enemies of our soul **don't** plant what we don't desire, therefore remember, **Pray without ceasing.**

CHAPTER 32

THE HOLY SPIRIT HELPS US IN OUR SPIRITUAL AWAKENING JOURNEY PART 1

As you will agree, spiritual awakening is a lifetime journey and process.

According to somernation.com, a **spiritual awakening** can generally be defined as a newfound awareness of a **spiritual** reality.

Scottjeffrey.com puts it this way. "Spiritual awakening is an **awakening** of a dimension of reality beyond the confines of the ego. (Mind) The ego is our exclusive sense of self or "I." This **awakening** occurs when, for whatever reason, the ego (mind) somehow let's go so that a Higher Self or **Spirit** can arise within."

Ego means "mind."

The Great Apostle Paul's main object was to get us on this **spiritual awakening journey.**

At the beginning of the book of **Galatians, in chapter 1 verse 1**, he describes himself as **Paul**, an **apostle (not of men**, but by **Jesus Christ, and God the Father**, who raised him from the dead).

It's fair to say **Apostle Paul's primary mentor was the Holy Spirit**, not men; he was called by **Jesus Christ**. Therefore, let's find out the **meaning of our Lord's name.**

The name *Jesus* is derived from the Hebrew name **Yeshua**, which is based on the **Semitic root y-š-ʕ (Hebrew: ישע)**, *meaning* "**to deliver; save, to rescue.**" **Yeshua,** and its longer form, **Yehoshua or Joshua,** is the literal **Hebrew** word for **Salvation.**

Christ means **the Power of God and the Wisdom of God (1 Corinthians 1:24).**

This Christ, the Power and Wisdom of God, must be formed in us; this is the **key to our salvation and to** being saved and rescued by **Jesus, our Lord.**

This awakening equals the manifestations of the sons of God. It is Christ formed in us. .

On the journey of **spiritual awakening,** some **vicinities (including religious)** and people will **hinder the process and one's progress**. We must always pray for **divine wisdom; this makes a lot of difference.**

God's wisdom will always direct our steps. I sincerely believe **the manifestation of the sons of God** must happen personally **(on a personal level with the Holy Spirit).**

Apostle Paul explains in **Galatians 4** who we are; that's why the **Christian faith is more than a motivational message.**

Motivational messages are fine and have their place, but it's about time for the world to see the **manifestation of the Sons of God.**

Technically, we might call ourselves **sons and daughters of God;** however, the truth is that **we grow into son-ship**. In other words, **we have to awaken, and this is a process with steps involved.**

Apostle Paul gives some insight into **being an heir of God** (sons and daughters of God).

Let's see Galatians 4 the Amplified titles of this Son-ship in Christ:

Now what I mean [when I talk about children and their guardians] is this: **as long as the heir is a child, he does not differ at all from a slave even though he is the [future owner and] master of all [the estate];**

2 but he is under [the authority of] guardians and household administrators *or* managers until the date set by his father [when he is of legal age].

3 So also we [whether Jews or Gentiles] when we were children (spiritually immature), were **kept like slaves under the elementary** [human-made religious or philosophical] teachings of the world.

4 But when [in God's plan] the proper time had fully come, **God sent His Son, born of a woman**, born under the [regulations of the] Law,

5 so that He might redeem *and* liberate those who were under the Law, that we [who believe] might be **adopted as sons [as God's children with all rights as fully grown members of a family].**

6 And because **you [really] are [His] sons, God has sent the Spirit of His Son into our hearts**, crying out, [a] **"Abba! Father!"**

7 Therefore you are no longer a slave (bond-servant), but a son; and if a son, then also an heir through [the gracious act of] God [through Christ].

But at that time, when you did not know [the true] God *and* were unacquainted with Him, you [Gentiles] **were slaves to those [pagan] things which by [their very] nature were not *and* could not be gods *at all*.**

9 Now, however, since you have come to **know [the true] God [through personal experience], or rather to be known by God**, how is it that you are **turning back again to the weak and worthless elemental**

principles [of religions and philosophies], to which you want to be enslaved all over again?

10 [For example,] you observe [particular] days and months and seasons and years.

11 I fear for you that perhaps I have labored [to the point of exhaustion] over you in vain.

Please allow me to show you the Voice version of Galatians 4: 1-11:

Listen. I am going to explain *how this all works:* When a **minor inherits** an estate *from his parents*, although he is the owner of everything, he is the same as **a slave.**

2 Until the day set by his father, the minor is subject to the authorities or guardians *whom his father put in charge.*

3 It is like that with us; there was a time when we were like children held under the elemental powers of this world.

4 When the right time arrived, God sent His Son into this world (born of a woman, subject to the Law)

5 **to free those who,** *just like Him,* were subject to the Law. **Ultimately He wanted us all to be adopted as sons and daughters.**

6 Because you are ***now part of God's family***, He sent the **Spirit of His Son into our hearts**; *and **the Spirit** calls out,* "Abba, Father."

7 You **no longer** have to live **as a slave** because you are **a child** *of God*. And since you are His child, **God guarantees** an inheritance *is waiting* for you.

"Abba" is an address spoken by children to their fathers expressing intimacy and respect. It would not be out-of-the-question to think of it as "Dad," or "Daddy."

8 During the time **before** you **knew God, you were slaves to powers that are not gods at all.**

9 But now, when you are just **beginning to know** *the one True* God—actually, *He is showing how* **completely** He knows you— *how can you turn back to weak and worthless idols made by men, icons of these spiritual powers?*

Haven't you **endured enough bondage to these** *breathless* **idols?**

10 **You are observing particular days, months,** *festival* **seasons, and years;**

11 you have me worried that I may have wasted my time laboring among you.

I find verse 10, fascinating. The apostle says you are observing particular days, and we call them **birthdays, festival seasons,** and **years.** We have **Christmas and Easter, which are PAGAN holidays,** and **we fit them around Jesus' birth and death.**

God wants CHRIST (His Power and Wisdom) **formed in us**. It's time we wake up.

From experience, I don't think religion can awaken a person. It's personal, and often, **God has to get our attention. We take our awakened state to eternity**; our soul comes to this **time and space reality to grow** (how much of God can be formed in us).

Let's read one of my favorite verses, Galatians 1: 10:

Am I now [trying to win the favor *and* **approval of men, or of God? Or am I seeking to please someone?** If I were still trying to be popular with men, I **would not** be a bond-servant of **Christ.**

Ultimately we are **bond servants to the Power & Wisdom of Go**d, which is on the inside of us, and **we must obey the directions of this incredible force.**

THE HOLY SPIRIT HELPS US IN OUR SPIRITUAL AWAKENING JOURNEY, PART 2

For the **Word of God** is living and active *and* **full of power** [making it operative, energizing, and effective]. It is sharper than any two-edged sword, penetrating as far as the division of the soul and spirit [the completeness of a person], and of both joints and marrow [the deepest parts of our nature], **exposing *and* judging the very thoughts and intentions of the heart. (Hebrews 4:12)**

Now in John 1:1, the Bible reads:

(The Deity of Christ) In the beginning [before all-time] was the **Word (Christ), and the Word was with God,** and the **Word was God Himself.** (Amplified).

Since we have established that for us to fully awake, **Christ must be formed in us,** and **Christ is the Word**, and the **Word is God**, then **God is formed in us**, and then see the **manifestation of the sons of God.**

The Word of God, which is God (Christ), when formed in us, we become living and active and full of power (Hebrews 4:12).

We also become **Psalm 82:6: we grow into it.** If you are wondering how one grows into becoming sons of God, the answer I can give is the **Holy Spirit.** This is also confirmed by the **Apostle John** in **1 John 2:27,** Amplified:

As for you, **the anointing [the special gift,** the preparation] which you received from Him remains **[permanently] in you**, and you **have no need for anyone to teach you.** But just as **His anointing teaches you [giving you insight through the presence of the Holy Spirit] about all things**, and **is true and is not a lie,** and just as His anointing has taught you, **you must remain in Him [being rooted in Him, knit to Him].**

The **Holy Spirit monitors our progress**, and He knows when we are ready for the **next level in God.** By now, I am sure we have come to the revelation and understanding that there are **levels in God and in His Word.**

The Holy Spirit reveals the next level of truth to us when we are **ready and when we can receive it.**

In as much as the enemy **(kingdom of darkness together with its zombie agents) is attacking** with all they have, the Holy Spirit is allowing it, and **its all part of the process.**

We know that **Christ is the power of God and the wisdom of God**, and we have come to the agreement that this **power comes from the Holy Spirit**, so we now need to look at the **wisdom of God.**

Before we look at how the word *wisdom* is used in the Bible about Jesus, let's see what the Lord says in **Psalm 14.**

The **opposite of wisdom is foolishness.** This is the Word of the Lord in Psalm 14. It is titled "**The Folly and Wickedness of Men.**" **Starting from verse 1:**

The [spiritually ignorant] fool has said in his heart, "There is no God."

They are corrupt, they have **committed repulsive *and* unspeakable deeds;**

There is no one who does good. (Amplified)

The New King James version reads Psalm 14 as follows:

The **fool has said in his heart,**

"*There is* no God."

They are corrupt,

They have done abominable works,

There is none who does good.

2 The Lord looks down from heaven upon the children of men,

To see if there are any who understand, who seek God.

3 They have **all turned aside,**

They have together **become corrupt;**

There is none who does good,

No, not one.

4 Have all the workers of iniquity no knowledge,

Who eat up my people *as* they eat bread,

And do not call on the Lord?

5 There they are **in great fear,**

For God *is* with the generation of the righteous.

6 You shame the counsel of the poor,

But the Lord *is* his refuge.

7 Oh,that the salvation of Israel *would come* out of Zion!

When the Lord brings back the captivity of His people,

Let Jacob rejoice *and* Israel be glad.

The enemy thinks he can win against God and His children, but I've got news for you: as long as God has stubborn sons and soldiers like me, we will not bow down, even if our last drop of blood depended on it.

Jesus Christ and Wisdom

Luke 2:40: "And the Child **(Jesus Christ)** continued to grow and become strong [in spirit], filled with **wisdom;** and the grace (favor, spiritual blessing) of God was upon Him."

As I indicated earlier, we grow into the things of the spirit. If **Jesus Christ had to grow, so do us. It's a process, and there are no shortcuts, nor is there mixing of power from the dark kingdom.**

Luke 2:52: "And **Jesus** kept **increasing in wisdom** and in stature, and in favor with **God and men."**

The word *increasing* **is defined** as **becoming greater in size**, amount, or degree, growing. We also should **expect to become greater in power and in favor with God and man.**

Matthew 13:54: "And after coming to [Nazareth] His hometown, He *began* teaching them in their synagogue, and they were astonished, and said, '**Where did this Man get this wisdom** and these miraculous powers [what is the source of His authority]?'"

When we begin to **awake and walk more closely with God/Holy Spirit, His wisdom becomes our wisdom as we start to become ONE.**

Mark 6:2, "When the Sabbath came, He began to teach in the synagogue, and the many listeners were astonished, saying, 'Where did this Man get these things, and **what is this wisdom given to Him,** and such miracles as these performed by His hands?'"

Again on the process of **becoming ONE with God, wisdom is automatically given to us**, furthermore, there are some instructions from the

Holy Spirit that are **personal;** hence, I can't share them. Also, the fact is, my many enemies would use the information against me. **The Holy Spirit gives us specific and individual instructions.**

Finally in Revelation 5:12, saying in a loud voice,

"Worthy *and* deserving is the Lamb that was **sacrificed to receive power** and riches and **wisdom** and might and honor and glory and blessing."

In following **Jesus Christ**, our **flesh must be sacrificed (slain)**, there are things that our **flesh desperately wants**, but the **Holy Spirit says no** (such **as sex before marriage)**. We are crucified with Christ, yet we live, but not us, but Christ lives within us. Amen.

Spiritual wisdom is foolishness to the WORLD because the **god of this world (Satan) has blinded their eyes.**

THE HOLY SPIRIT HELPS US ON OUR SPIRITUAL AWAKENING JOURNEY, PART 3

Before I start on the wisdom of God formed in us, I want to **emphasize** that we are created in the **image and likeness of God**.

We can see this in the **Genesis 1:26:** "Then let us make man in Our image according to Our likeness and let them have dominion."

The **first mention principle**: God indicates in the **first mention** of a **subject the truth** with which that subject stands connected in the mind of God.

According to the **Voice translation**, it reads, "Now let Us conceive *a new creation—*humanity*—made* in Our image, *fashioned* according to Our likeness. And let *Us grant* them **authority over all the Earth.**"

In case you are wondering what the **verse means by word *Us*,** the **amplified version helps answer the question** in its version of Genesis 1:26,

Then God said, **"Let Us (Father, Son, Holy Spirit)** make man in Our image, according to Our likeness [not physical, but a **spiritual personality and moral likeness**], and let them have complete authority

God then formed us from dust in **Genesis 2:7.**

In other words, **God created us before he formed us.**

Going back to Genesis 1:26, it says "in **our image and likeness.**"

If **God is a Spirit** (image), **we are spirit**; according to the **Christian faith,** so we must be **born again** before we can come into the **mysterious awareness. John 3:21: "Jesus answered him**, I assure you, most solemnly I tell you, that unless a person is **born again** (anew, from above), he cannot ever see **(know, be acquainted with, and experience) the Kingdom of God.**"

Let's look at some definitions:

1. **Likeness** –the fact or quality of being alike; resemblance.

2. **According to** –in conformity with (Merriam Webster)

We were **created** before we were **formed in our mother's womb,** and as **God told Prophet Jeremiah,** He **(God)** knew us before we were formed in our mother's womb.

Reading between the lines from the **Old Testament and the New Testament,** I believe we are **created once (our soul),** but we could be **formed in several wombs at different times.**

For instance, **when Jesus asked His disciples, "Who do people say I am?"** they said **John the Baptist, Elijah, Jeremiah, one of the proph**ets. **Jesus never rebuked their theology** but said, **"Who do you say I am?"** Then Peter said, **"You are the Christ."**

I know folks will be saying, "How about **Hebrews 9:27,** which says 'it's appointed for man to die once then the judgment'?"

Notice the verse says **it is appointed for MAN** to die once, but we have failed to realize **we are not man;** we are **soul and spirit. The flesh (man) dies once,** but the **journey of our soul continues until we have fully awakened into the image and likeness of God.**

To prove my point, we know that the **Bible said Elijah would come again before the Messiah came. Bible scholars** agree **that Elijah didn't**

come as Elijah, but he came as **John the Baptist with the power and spirit of Elijah.**

I saw a verse in the **Bible** yesterday that I had **never seen before,** and it's **Psalm 17:15b (NKJ): "I shall be satisfied when I awake in Your likeness."**

Therefore, we have to **awaken into God.** This is the **purpose of every Christian.** A lot of folks in the **Church** are **just doing religion, and** most of them are **fast asleep.**

The **devil deceives folks into the wrong objective,** to **create a name (the folks sell their soul – stupid and dumb)** for **yourself,** and to **die like a mere man. People die still asleep; that is a waste.**

It's the **greatest deception** in the **history of man,** and many people are still **falling for the trick – what would a person give in exchange of his soul?** Our soul is meant to **prosper** and not be **SOLD.**

We have recognized that **Jesus Christ** came to **save** and **awaken us** so that **Christ** (the power and wisdom of God) may be **formed in us.**

There is **NO way we can awake without the Holy Spirit**; even the spirit of wisdom is a **gift of the Holy Spirit.** To **awaken in God's likeness**, we need the **power and wisdom of God.** Everybody will agree that the source of power is from the **Holy Spirit**, but how do we get the **Wisdom of God** formed in us?

Several practical ways are to **pray in the Holy Spirit (speak in tongues) regularly** and to **meditate on wisdom verses in the Word of God.**

Let's look at a few verses on wisdom:

Job 28:28

Behold, <u>the fear of the Lord, that is wisdom</u>, and to depart from evil is understanding. <u>(NKJV)</u>

Psalm 111:10

The fear of the LORD is the beginning of wisdom; all who follow his precepts have a good understanding. To him belongs eternal praise. (NIV)

King David, at his best, **understood what life was about**, and we see this in **Psalm 17.15b:** "I will be satisfied when I awake in your likeness." This **sums up our purpose here on Earth**. It's doesn't stop here, though. **King Solomon shared with us the advice his father King David gave him in regard to wisdom**, in **Proverbs 4:**

A Father's Instruction

Hear, O children, the instruction of a father,

And pay attention [and be willing to learn] so that you may gain understanding *and* intelligent discernment.

For I give you right doctrine;

Do not turn away from my instruction.

When I was a **son** with my father **(David),**

Tender and the only son in the sight of my mother **(Bathsheba),**

He taught me and said to me,

"Let your heart hold fast my words;

Keep my commandments and live.

"Get **[skillful and godly] wisdom!** Acquire understanding [actively seek spiritual discernment, mature comprehension, and logical interpretation]!

Do not forget nor turn away from the **words of my mouth**.

"Do not turn away from her **(Wisdom)** and she will guard *and* protect you;

Love her, and she will watch over you.

"The **beginning of wisdom** is Get [skillful and godly] wisdom [it is preeminent]!

And with all your **acquiring, get understanding** [actively seek spiritual discernment, mature comprehension, and logical interpretation].

"**Prize wisdom** [and exalt her], and **she will exalt you**;

She will **honor you** if you **embrace her**.

"She will place on your head a garland of **grace**;

She will present you with a crown of beauty *and* glory."

Hear, my son, and accept my sayings,

And the years of your life will be many.

I have instructed you in the way of [skillful and godly] wisdom;

I have led you in upright paths.

When you walk, your steps will not be impeded [for your path will be clear and open];

And when you run, you will not stumble.

Take hold of instruction; [actively seek it, grip it firmly and] do not let go.

Guard her, for she is your life.

Do not enter the path of the wicked,

And do not go the way of evil men.

Avoid it, do not travel on it;

Turn away from it and pass on.

For the wicked cannot sleep unless they do evil;

And they are deprived of sleep unless they make someone stumble *and* fall.

For they eat the bread of wickedness

And drink the wine of violence.

But the path of the just (righteous) is like the light of dawn,

That shines brighter and brighter until [it reaches its full strength and glory in] the perfect day.

The way of the wicked is like [deep] darkness;

They do not know over what they stumble.

My son, pay attention to my words *and* be willing to learn;

Open your ears to my sayings.

Do not let them escape from your sight;

Keep them in the center of your heart.

For they are life to those who find them,

And healing *and* health to all their flesh.

Watch over your heart with all diligence,

For from it *flow* the springs of life.

Put away from you a deceitful (lying, misleading) mouth,

And put devious lips far from you.

Let your eyes look directly ahead [toward the path of moral courage]

And let your gaze be fixed straight in front of you [toward the path of integrity].

Consider well *and* watch carefully the path of your feet,

And all your ways will be steadfast *and* sure.

Do not turn away to the right nor to the left [where evil may lurk];

Turn your foot from [the path of] evil.

We all have a **choice with whom we follow and serve**, but let me leave you with the **words of Joshua: "As for me and my house we shall serve the Lord, and our primary objective is to awake to God's likeness."**

Seeking the **light (Kingdom of God)** and awakening in **God's image** and likeness **does not come without a fight.**

The **kingdom of darkness** will attack you with all they have, but just remember Christ – the **power and wisdom of God** – is sufficient to help you along this journey.

An important truth to remember is that the **Kingdom of God** suffers **violence, and violence takes by force (Matthew11:12).** So let's be **STRONG** and **fight the good fight of FAITH. Amen.**

THE HOLY SPIRIT HELPS US IN OUR AWAKENING JOURNEY, PART 4

When I started with this project, I didn't know where it was going to lead.

However, I knew one thing was **certain: the Holy Spirit** separates **Christianity** from all other **religions**, especially in this **21st century, where anything goes.**

To **fully comprehend** the person of the **Holy Spirit**, one must have an **intimate relationship** with the **Holy Spirit.**

We have heard the saying "the **Bible is the manual for life**," which is a correct statement, but to add to that, **the Holy Spirit is the companion for every serious Christian.**

The **Holy Spirit** takes out the **mechanics of religion** from the **Christian faith.** Unfortunately, there are a lot of churches that are very mechanical, as they don't allow the **Holy Spirit to have a free flow.**

When one starts to **awaken to the likeness of God**, one quickly sees the **darkness that surrounds**; it becomes **conspicuous.**

When one begins to awaken, there is a **sad truth** that has to **be embraced: you can't trust anybody, not even your blood. Folks will do anything for a buck; they will sell you out and betray you like Judas. Hosanna today, crucify tomorrow.**

The obvious wise thing to do when there is a **lack of trust** is to **break away,** as one has to **break from the old before the new can begin.**

However, **break away in love and wisdom** as the **primary reason** for this action is to **protect one's soul.**

This spiritual journey is **crucial for eternity,** as the **battle for one's SOUL rages on**, and my spirit goes to **Acts 20:32,** and it is the **Word of God** and the **Holy Spirit** that we **genuinely need** and can **trust.**

Acts 20:32 (Message version) goes as follows: "Now, I'm turning you over to **God, our marvelous God** whose **gracious Word** can make you **into what he wants you to be** and give you everything **you could possibly need** in this community of holy friends."

If a person is **willing to stand for Christ, amid so-called Christians** and the **parts of the Body of Christ** that are **selling out, tangible and intangible (visible and invisible) rewards** await such people **in both this time and space and also in Heaven.**

The Christian walk gets **tough,** I must confess, but once one has a **revelation of the TRUTH,** there is **no turning back,** and **if people don't want to go with you,** then **cut the suckers loose.** I know it might **feel and often seems that one is alone,** but **2 Chronicles 16:9** reminds us that the **eyes of the Lord move to and fro throughout the earth so He may support those whose hearts are completely His.**

People **can't be forced** to follow the **light (Jesus Christ).** Either you got the revelation or not. **Thank goodness** I am not an **evangelist,** as I certainly **don't have the patience to convince anyone about our Lord Jesus Christ.** There are different **levels in Christianity**, and these levels have equal importance. **Nevertheless, my message is that the Christian faith and Christians NEED the Holy Spirit more than ever.**

The **Holy Spirit has made the difference in my life;** that's simply the **secret to my survival**, and that's why I will **never trade nor even**

accommodate any other religion. There is something about the presence of the **Holy Spirit and the glory of His goodness.**

I find writing very interesting; I believe it's the same writing lyrics. Sometimes, one doesn't know where the art is leading. I say this because I didn't know the end of this project would lead to the **awakening of the human soul.** Let's look at my favorite Apostle – **The Great Apostle Paul.** From his conversion on the way to **Damascus, Saul became Paul,** and this **incredible man of God fully awoke.**

Apostle Paul gave revelations that even his **fellow apostles were dumbfounded by.** I am **astonished myself from his epistles**; not only is he a **brilliant spiritual write**r, but his revelation always makes me want to **jump in amazement.** I can s**ometimes feel what he felt as he wrote his letters, but I still have a long way to go.**

For instance, Philippians 1:21: "For to me, **to live is Christ** [He is my source of joy, my reason to live] and to **die is gain** [for I will be with Him in eternity].

Let's **break this down** a little bit: **to awaken means Christ is formed in us – the power and wisdom of God.** This **feeling is exhilarating.** At this level of consciousness, **one doesn't care whether one is here in time or space or with the Lord.**

At this level of awareness, **one has zero fear of death, absolutely ZERO.** In this experience, one has **tasted and seen the love and goodness of God,** and one can **NEVER EVER TURN BACK from such glorious presence of God.**

So, to all you **folks who want a person to settle for something less,** all I can say is that **I have no choice but to CUT YOU OFF and BREAK AWAY.** I want to experience what **God has ordained for me to experience; I want the BEST OF GOD in ETERNITY.**

I **do pray that God opens your blind eyes**, and **may God** give you the **grace** needed to **awake**.

Nobody **can complete with the Precious Holy Spirit;** hence, it would be **DUMB and stupid to follow you.**

I know your **tricks and can discern your motives and moves**, and you **can't compare to the incomparable POWER and BENEFITS of walking with God and the PRECIOUS HOLY SPIRIT.**

I am aware of all your evil witchcraft, but I have news for you: **KAR-MA is going to get you and your household. Galatians 6:7 (Ampli-fied):** "Do not be deceived, **God is not mocked** [He will not allow Him-self to be ridiculed, nor treated with contempt nor allow His precepts to be scornfully set aside]; for **whatever a man sows**, this *and* this only is **what he will reap."**

To my fellow serious Christians, it's time to awake.

Let's be like the psalmist King David and say, "I shall be satisfied when I awake in Your likeness" **(Psalm 17: 15b).**

CHAPTER 33

TIME TO CHANGE OUR WAYS—THE WORD OF THE LORD

When I started this book, I couldn't have predicted that the world would be in the position it's in today, neither did I **pick the topic**, but it was the Lord who **laid it on my heart**.

The book **started early last year.** Now looking back, I can see why the Lord laid the topic on my heart.

God knows all things, including the **horrible coronavirus** we are facing today. No one could have forecasted the **effect the coronavirus would have on the world** or anything that would cause a **worldwide dilemma** we are facing today.

One thing is for sure: **nothing catches God off guard or by surprise.**

According to the **Book of Ecclesiastes** in the Bible, the **first verse of Chapter 3 says: "Everything that happens in this World occurs at the time God chooses"** (Good News translation), and it's fair to say nothing happens on **Earth without God's permission** because **Psalm 24 verse 1 says,** "The earth is the Lord's, and the fullness of it, the world, and those who dwell in it."

God puts a hedge of protection around His people. Job 1:10 says, "Have You not put a hedge about him and his house and all that he has, on every side?"

The hedge of protection can be removed for various reasons. Job's hedge of protection was removed because he was about to be tested.

According to the **Revelations 3: 10b,** "The hour of trial (testing) which is coming on the whole World to try those who dwell upon the earth."

May I point out that the hour of trial (testing) is already here, and it's called Corona virus Covid 19.

The hedge of protection can also be removed when we **decide not to follow God's rules, and people have missed the mark by living in SIN.**

Sin and partaking from the **table of the kingdom of darkness will break the hedge of protection**, and the enemy can penetrate and attack.

On a personal level, there are things **I CANNOT** do, even in as much as my flesh desperately wants to do such things. The reason I can't do such activities is that I know I am a **target for the devil and his dark kingdom**, and by doing what **God says I shouldn't do**, I would be giving the devil license to overpower and torment me.

It's just like a person who buys a **piece of equipment** and decides NOT follow the **rules in the manual;** hence, whatever happens, as a result, is not the **manufacturer's fault** but the fault of the person who chose not to follow the instructions in the manual.

The **same analogy** that applies to an **individual is applicable to countries** and to the world at large. If people allow secret societies that worship Satan (darkness) to take over the world, then the hedge of protection will be broken. **The enemy of our soul will have permission to do whatever.**

In Deuteronomy 3: 19, we see another warning from God: beware lest you lift up your eyes to the heavens, and when you **see the sun, moon, and stars, even all the host of the heavens, you be drawn away and worship them** and serve them, things which the Lord your God has allotted to all nations under the whole heaven.

How many people **worship the sun, moon, etc.**? If you do, **God warned us NOT** to. **The 24th verse of Deuteronomy 4 says, "For the Lord your God is a consuming fire, a jealous God."**

We can see how we have missed the mark. **A high percentage of the Church is lukewarm, with their seeker-friendly messages.**

Preachers, what happened? Did you sell out? Were you more **interested in your pockets than in preaching the accurate Word of God?** Why did you **not warn the people**? A lot of you preachers **often boast over how many members you have, but what do you preach in your churches.**

Whatever **happened or is happening, we brought it upon ourselves**. How can some members of the Church of Jesus Christ be **involved in the practice of dark magic?** Such s**o-called ministers** should **NEVER** be allowed to **preach the Gospel again.**

The question is, so what do we do now?

The first thing we have to do is, **repent and turn back to God. Repent means** "to feel or express sincere regret or remorse about one's wrongdoing or sin."

I give **credit** to **President Trump** for calling for a **day of prayer**, and **God will honor that** and **give necessary wisdom** on how to deal with the coronavirus.

Folks need to repent and live according to the rules of God and stop the **killing of innocent babies.**

That's why countries must have **pro-life presidents/leaders** because the **killing of innocent babies (the sacrifice of babies) is an abomination to God.** This will cause the hedge of protection to be broken, and consequently, **we will pay the price**.

It is interesting that China, one of the top countries that persecute the Christian faith, is where this horrible virus originated.

Another thing that needs to be removed from our society is **sorcery and witchcraft.**

The rise of dark magic is alarming. I read some time ago that the fastest growing religion is **witchcraft.** A lot of young people are being recruited and initiated into the dark kingdom. **God is not happy with this.**

In **Exodus 22:18**, God made it clear what should happen to those who practice dark magic, so repent and STOP the witchcraft, **so God can heal the land as we pray.**

2 Chronicles 7:14 reads, "If My people, who are called by My name, shall humble themselves, pray, seek, crave, *and* require of necessity My face and turn from their **wicked ways**, then will I hear from heaven, forgive their sin, and heal their land."

The wicked ways in the verse mostly come from those who practice **dark magic, sorcery and witchcraft.**

God said that His people should always cover themselves with the **Blood of Jesus** and **pray in the Holy Spirit,** as this would **intensify one's faith and authority over the coronavirus.**

In as much as **the incomparable power of a Christian is the Holy Spirit,** the realization of such power on a Christian **is not automatic**; a person **NEEDS to be baptized in the Holy Spirit with the evidence of speaking and praying in tongues.**

The praying in tongues has to be done **regularly,** as this is the secret to accessing this **incredible POWER.**

When our **Lord Jesus Christ was arrested**, His **disciples ran away and deserted the Lord.**

After Jesus' resurrection, He appeared to His disciples and instructed them **how to receive the Holy Spirit.** After receiving this power, they became as **bold as lions, turned the world upside down, and spread the Gospel all over the world, and we are benefiting from that today.**

Stay well. Stay healthy.

Remember, **Jesus Chris**t is the **Light** and **Saviour** of the world.

God bless you.

REFERENCES

Editors at History.com (2009) 'The Reformation'
Available at http://www.history.com/topics/reformation
Accessed: 11/November 2019.

Editorial Staff (2019) 'The Discernment of Spirits'
Available at http://www.Christianity.com
Accessed: 03/November 2019

Faith Mechanic (2017) 'Peace is the Emotion of Faith'
Available at http://hopefaithprayer.com/peace-is/
Accessed: 03/ November 2019

Karuvilla, C (2005) 'Wolf Hall'
Available at http://www.huffpost.com/entry/wolf-hall
Accessed: 30/April 2019

Kuhlman, K. The Greatest Power in the World. Bridge – Logos Publication, 1997

Kuhlman, K. I Believe in Miracles. Bridge – Logos Publication, 1992

Lake, J G. Your Power in the Holy Spirit. Whitaker House, 2010

Robbins, T. (2008) Recognizing prompts of the Holy Spirit
Available at http:// www.happyhealthyandprosperous.com
Accessed Date. 03/November 2019

Wigglesworth, S. Smith Wigglesworth on Faith. Whitaker House 1998